Lisa Marie

Presley

Memoir

A Life of Fame, Music, and Heartache

Anthony N Dopson

Table of Content

Chapter 1: Upstairs at Graceland

I believed my father had the ability to manipulate the weather.

He was a god to me. A chosen human being.

He had that thing that allowed you to see his soul. If he was in a bad mood, it was bad outside; if it was storming, it meant he was going to go off. Back then, I felt he could create a storm.

Make him happy and make him laugh—that was my entire universe. If I knew something was humorous to him, I would do everything I could to get some mileage out of it and entertain him. When we left Graceland, the fans would invariably say, "Alvis! Alvis!" in their Southern accents. When I mocked someone doing it, he burst out laughing and died. He thought it was the funniest thing he had ever heard.

Another day, I was sleeping in my hamburger-shaped bed—a massive black-and-white fur bed with steps coming up to it—and he was sitting next to me in a chair, so I asked him, "How much money do you have?" He tumbled out of his chair, laughing. I couldn't see why that was so humorous.

I was quite connected to him. Our relationship was closer than I had previously admitted to anyone.

He adored me and was completely devoted to me, going above and above for me despite everything else. He gave me his everything, more than he could give anybody else.

I dreaded him, too. He was intense, and you did not want him to become furious with you. If I ever offended him or made him angry, I felt like everything was coming to an end. I couldn't deal with it.

My mother was an Air Force brat. She met my father at the age of fourteen, and her parents approved it. That was a different time.

Back then, women were admitted to the hospital while in labor. They'd pass out and wake up with a baby. She entered the hospital looking elegant and attractive, and when she awoke, she was handed a child.

My mother informed me that she had considered falling off her horse to induce a miscarriage.

She did not want to gain weight. She felt it wouldn't be a good appearance for her as Elvis' wife. There were so many women after him, all of them stunning. She wants his complete attention. She was so angry about being pregnant that she first ate only apples and eggs and never gained much weight. I was a pain in her ass from the start, and I always had the impression that she did not want me.

I believe in energy in utero, so perhaps I already sensed her desire to get rid of me. She eventually decided to retain me, but she didn't have the best mother instincts back then.

That could be what is wrong with me.

When I was younger, I would frequently watch my mother do her makeup. Her bathroom has two sinks separated by a large vanity. My mother had more makeup than any little girl could imagine: MAC and Kevyn Aucoin, drawers upon drawers of brushes and lip pencils, eye shadows, and Spice, the most renowned MAC lip color. She would line her lips with the Cupid's bow she adored and which we all got from her father, peering into a small mirror on the vanity, and I thought they were flawless. To me, she was the world's most beautiful woman.

I looked at her and asked, "How old are you?"

I had never considered her age before. She chuckled and announced, "I'm twenty-eight."

How young that was.

My mother fundamentally believed she was broken, unlovable, and not beautiful. She had a strong sense of unworthiness, and I never understood why. I have spent my entire life trying to figure out the solution. My mother was a difficult and misunderstood lady.

In my family, young girls have a long history of becoming moms; my great-grandmother, grandmother, and mother all had their first infants when they were still babies.

As I grew older, I wished I could have been my mother's and grandmother's mother. I began to realize what all of the young mothers were missing.

I was told that my birth tale was sweet. My father, like everyone else, was extremely nervous. They went through a lot of dress rehearsals to figure out the quickest path to the hospital. They had run a few tests and everything was good. Then Jerry Schilling, one of my father's oldest friends, nearly drove to the incorrect hospital.

Then, I was born.

My mother wanted to appear good for my father, so she applied artificial eyelashes before he walked in to visit us. However, she was still high and attached them to the mirror rather than to her eyelids.

After that, there was a news conference; my mother and father stepped out of the hospital, waved, and everyone took pictures. So, from the moment I was born, the press was present.

Then they drove me home to Graceland.

Tom and Ruth Moore, a doctor and his wife, founded Graceland in 1939. The land was given to the family by the wife's aunt Grace, so they called it after her. Elvis liked the name so much that he kept it when he bought the ten-thousand-square-foot house and fourteen acres for $102,000 in 1957.

Back then, the area was still rural; there was nothing five miles south of Memphis. Graceland was not even a part of the city proper until 1969.

Elvis' grandmother's room was upstairs, but after his mother died, Minnie Mae moved downstairs. When Priscilla became pregnant in 1967, Elvis and Priscilla built an upstairs nursery, which served as my mother's room.

Graceland does not appear to be much of a mansion in comparison to modern homes; visitors are frequently struck by its diminutive size. But when Elvis bought it, it was more than just a house; it signified so much more than size and land. Until 1953, the Presleys lived in modest circumstances. Graceland was the tangible embodiment of the most spectacular American dream come true. Elvis was a small-town boy from a poor family, yet he had somehow grown into a godlike figure, the world's biggest star. Nonetheless, he remained a Southern kid who only got to buy his loving Mama a large old house.

The entire region smells like the South, especially during the summer. There is a pleasant summer breeze and fireflies at night.

Beautiful trees surround the house, including magnolias, elms, willow oaks, red maples, pecans, and black cherries.

When you walk through the main door, the living room is directly on your right, with its iconic stained-glass blue peacocks, single TV, and grand piano. The stairs in front of you go to Elvis' and my mother's bedrooms. The dining room is on the left and features plush floor-to-ceiling draperies atop a black marble floor. The kitchen is located on the first floor, as is the famous Jungle Room, which features shag carpeting and an indoor waterfall. The pool room is located below and has cushioned walls and ceilings. It serves as another hiding area, similar to the Jungle Room.

The stables, racquetball court, and a swing set owned by my mother may all be found behind Graceland.

My brother, Ben, and I grew up visiting Graceland over the holidays. At the end of each day, when the visitor tours were finished, we'd stay out in the house with our family, eating enormous dinners and racing about, jumping on couches and playing pool. Graceland was only our home while we were there, despite the fact that it was open to the public. It's bizarre and incredible to have your family's history recorded forever in the very location where it all occurred.

It's as if the entire life that was lived in that house—all the joy, tears, music, grief, and love—is still being replayed, down the stairs and in the walls.

I can feel my ancestors there.

His bedroom had large double vinyl black and gold doors that led to a little hallway, and my bedroom was just around the corner. When I got upstairs, I had to walk through his bedroom to get to mine. If the vinyl doors were closed, it signified he was sleeping. If they were open and I was up to no good, as I frequently was, I had to sneak past. But anytime the doors were open, I always looked inside to see what he was up to. He'd either be watching TV, talking to others, or reading.

My father had bought a house across from the pasture for my grandfather. My father was nocturnal, and every now and then he would wake me up, put me in a golf cart, and drive me over there to see Vernon, who was never prepared for it. We'd hang out for an hour or two before driving back home.

I couldn't get away with much when Vernon was present. He seemed more authoritative to me. I was not close to him. I would avoid him at any cost. I wished I had a different relationship with my grandfather. I just sort of hid from him.

Those night rides to Vernon, on the other hand, were simply a chance for my father and me to enjoy some alone time.

My father was very Southern.

No one says "goddamn" the way a Southerner does, with the correct soul and inflection. When done correctly, it's humorous. I overheard that all the time. My father and all of his buddies stated the same thing.

I wanted to go to the pet store, so my father shut it down one night and drove me there with his entourage. We each got to choose a pet. My dad chose a Pomeranian named Edmund, but I chose a small white fluffy puppy. A little later, I was in my room, and they had just brought his breakfast up to his room, as they always do. Then I heard "GODDAMN!" quite loudly. I rushed into his room, and he exclaimed, "That goddamn dog just stole my bacon!" Edmund had leaped into his bed, grabbed a slice of bacon, and ran downstairs. He was furious about the dog. Edmund became my aunt Delta's dog after that.

Other times, I'd be in my room watching TV when I heard "GODDAMN IT!" and went down the hall to his room to find out what was going on.

"GODDAMN IT!" I can't sneeze; I need to sneeze but can't!" I remember him saying something once before finally sneezing.

I had two cupboards full of stuffed animals in my room, and one day I thought I spotted something in there—maybe a mouse or a rat or something—which terrified me. So I ran to get my father.

"Daddy, something's in my room!"

My father collected his nightstick and cane, entered my room, and closed the door behind him. Then all I heard was banging and thrashing noises, with him saying, "Goddamn son of a bitch!" He was pounding the shit out of the stuffed animals, trying to find this thing, whatever it was, but it kept scurrying away. He eventually killed it, but no one moved it, and there was a horrible odor in there for about a month.

Another time, when I was in my room, I heard another "Goddamn son of a bitch!" from the front of the house. There was a booming gunshot.

When I ran downstairs, I discovered my father sitting in a lounge chair beneath a tree. A snake was coming down the tree and about to bite his foot, so he shot it.

Later, I needed to have a tonsillectomy. My father was also there in the hospital during that time. I recall being handed ice cream—which obviously no child would object to—but it was uncomfortable to eat anything, so I made a face every time I had to swallow. My father was sitting next to my hospital bed, waiting for me to swallow before he started laughing.

He thought that face was hilarious.

Her father called her Yisa. When he spoke to my mother, he replaced all l's with y's.

I was rocking my daughter, Tupelo, to sleep the other night, and I found myself calling her "itty-bitty" and singing to her, Mama's little baby loves shortnin', shortnin', and I stopped and thought, I literally haven't heard this song since I was a baby, and I realized in that moment that all of these phrases and things I use, and the things I say to my daughter, are the ways my mom spoke to me. She had gotten them directly from her father, from the South, and all of them are still alive." She mothered my baby through me. Whenever I go to the South and hear the Memphis accent, I feel a need, a nostalgia for something I never lived. I've never lived in Memphis, but something inside of me does.

Once the gates were locked, Graceland was like its own city, with its own authority. My father was the chief of police, and everyone was ranked. There were a few laws and rules, but basically none.

It was freedom.

My dad got me my own golf cart, which was baby blue and had my name on the side, which was a big deal to me.

There were a lot of carts, and my friends and I used to rip up the lawn with them, collide with each other head-on, or try to "decapitate" them by running into a tree branch. The entire day was a demolition derby. I would drive at full speed into a fence, and the next morning it appeared as if nothing had happened; the fence had been totally repaired.

There was a shed across the lawn in the backyard. My father used it for target practice with his rifles and firearms, but it was later utilized to store firecrackers for unknown reasons. Dad and his friends would shoot firecrackers at each other. One day, Dad lit one on top of a box of them, and they all burst at the same moment. The entire shed went up in flames. Sometimes I can't believe no one died up there. I don't know how we got away unscathed. Perhaps there was a spiritual being hovering over that place, that vortex.

Downstairs, there was a room with cloth on the walls, a pool table, and a bedroom reserved for any vagrant Memphis Mafia member present that night. Charlie Hodge resided in it. David Stanley also lived there. That zone had its own vortex. There were never-ending cigarettes, dirty magazines, cards, and novels. I was all about the nasty publications.

My father once hurled a stink bomb down the steps into that area and then locked the doors, preventing anyone from leaving. I just followed along with whatever he was doing. I'd play pool with my pals down there, and then we'd turn off the lights and throw pool balls at each other, having pool-stick fights in the darkness. Play hide-and-seek. It was open season in that room. The country of shenanigans.

I used to run over people's feet with the golf cart before taking off. One day, I was tearing up the backyard with the cart, and someone told me to stop, and I said, "I'll tell my father when he wakes up." Another time, someone told me that I couldn't do something while on the golf cart, and I said, "I'll tell my father that your wife..." I wish I could remember what I said that his wife had done.

I was wild.

One day, when I asked for a chocolate cake, one of the cooks said, "No, your father's sick, he can't have that," and I said, "I'm telling my daddy you're fired."

I was four.

For many years, Elvis's original chefs would cook for us when we were at Graceland. My mother would have them cook everything she loved, all the things she ate with her father growing up: fried chicken and catfish, hush puppies and greens, banana pudding. When we came to town, the staff would always have our golf carts waiting, and after dinner, we'd go outside and wreak havoc on the lawns—we rarely drove on the road.

This was a family custom.

Billy Idol, Guns N' Roses, and Pat Benatar were her teen idols, so my mother was overjoyed when Billy Idol came to Graceland. They were off someplace on the grounds when my mother ran in, breathless.

"I just inadvertently hurled Billy Idol from the back of my golf cart!" she exclaimed, laughing uncontrollably.

I was on the run since my father slept all day, and I was accompanied by two pals who could have been Joe Esposito's children, my friend Laura, or my cousin Deana; I wish I could recall.

I was in a cute little outfit in my golf cart, sitting at the very edge of the seat so I could reach the pedals, and I was out back of Graceland, heading toward the trailers where part of my family lives, when someone stopped me.

"He's up and he wants to see you."

Damn, it's just two or three p.m., and he's not supposed to be up yet. Every possible thing I'd ever done ran through my mind. What has he discovered? Someone has told him something, and I'm going to kill whoever told me.

"We're in deep trouble," I told my companions. "I don't know what it's about yet, but he wants me right now, which is a problem."

I started crying as I walked toward the house, and so did my pals.

We made our way upstairs, and my father was seated in his customary spot on his bed, lying back on one of those arm-shaped pillows, twitching his leg or shaking his head, and rocking constantly.

He told us to sit down and then took out three small parcels, one for me, one for a friend, and one for another friend.

I opened mine, and it was a gorgeous ring adorned with a flower of diamonds. Each of us received a ring, with one buddy receiving emeralds and another receiving rubies.

It was so gorgeous, but I felt so guilty; he had only wanted us to hang out with him and talk. My conscience was eating me alive.

My mother told my father twenty minutes before he was supposed to walk onstage in Las Vegas, "I'm leaving," despite the fact that he still had to play.

I was four years old when my parents broke up, but I remained close to my father. I knew how much he appreciated me, how much he loved me, and how much I despised leaving him. I despised traveling to my mother's new home in Los Angeles, which he bought to be closer to me.

When I was in L.A., he would call at all hours of the night to chat to me or leave a message on my phone. I was taking piano lessons at the time, and he would want to hear them, so my mother would place the phone on the piano so he could hear me play.

I would do whatever he asked of me. I would sing, I would dance; I didn't like singing, but I knew it made him happy, so I did it; he wanted me to learn "Greensleeves" on the piano, so I did; he could have said, "Chop both of your feet off," and I would have done it.

Only to make him happy.

Dad and his mother, Gladys, had been so close, but she loved him so much that she drank herself to death worrying about him. She couldn't bear him being away in the army--he went to Germany--and she died as a result. This left my father with his own demons, and he acted out on them.

Every part of me wants to numb out and do the same damned thing.

My father gave me a horse, and I don't think it was for any special event. He was leading me through Graceland, right past the house, and everyone was delighted, making a ruckus, and Dodger was saying, "What the hell is going on out there?"" At that point, the horse halted and decided to waste himself just outside Dodger's door. It was unusual for her to get out of her chair, but she was able to do so, and she began to get up to see what was going on in the hallway.

My father was worried.

"Oh my God, we've gotta get out of here!" he said. "Clean it up quickly before she comes out!"

Then it was a frenzied rush to get the poop off the floor and the horse out of the house; as quickly as he could, he led me around to the front, made a circle, and we snuck out the back door before Dodger could find us.

Dodger had a daughter, Delta Mae Biggs, my aunt Delta, who took care of Dodger but was also a diabetic alcoholic, so she was a wild card. She had a terrible mouth and was very vocal about everything, but she was very, very hilarious.

Aunt Delta was put in charge of me for a while, but she couldn't control me; no matter what she said to me, I wouldn't listen. She'd just say, "Yeah, you little son of a bitch," and give up on me.

Aunt Delta always claimed that my cousin Patsy, who was a double first cousin, was my genuine surrogate mother.

One day, my aunt Delta and Patsy were fighting in the kitchen, and Delta pulled out a knife.

"I'll cut your guts out," Delta stated.

Patsy responded, "Well goddamn get over here and do it," but Delta wasn't going to do it; that was simply how they communicated.

My father had given Delta his Pomeranian, Edmund, who became her watchdog and protector. If you came anywhere near her room, that dog would start barking, growling, and going crazy, and you could hear her cursing at him to shut up from behind the door. She'd get in her bathrobe and take him out several times a day, clutched in her right arm. Later, when the tours started coming through, she'd still walk through the house in her bathrobe, carrying Edmund, and run into the viDelta and respond, "Oh hell no, she died."

Delta knew how much I adored Elton John, so she got me some of his records for Christmas. My father saw me open the gift, said, "That's nice," and went through the swinging doors that led from the dining room into the kitchen. Later, I discovered that in the kitchen, he asked Aunt Delta, "Why did you get her those records? Who the heck is this son of a bitch that she wants to hear?"

"She likes him," Delta replied.

Soon after, before one of his gigs, my father saw Elton backstage because he needed to meet this person whose recordings I was listening to. Elton and I have been laughing about it ever since.

A year later, on my ninth birthday, my mother arranged for me to visit Elton's house, where he showed me his clothing, closet, and boots. He was really sweet, and we had tea.

When I was in Memphis, I would wake up around two p.m. at Graceland and get everyone ready to play. I had friends up there who lived with my grandparents, or cousins who lived in trailers in the back. I would ask for French fries or grits for breakfast, get my golf cart, and we'd go for the day.

I would eat French fries for three days in a row or go 10 days without taking a bath.

My father would eventually wake up, and I'd get the call that I was to go upstairs because he wanted to see me. I'd go and hang out with him in his room, where there were enough people and things going on that there was never a moment of boredom. I'd just sit up there, and he'd talk to me and ask what I was doing while he watched one of his seventeen televisions or listened to records.

My father loved to have fun, and he wanted everyone else to have fun with him, and he loved to laugh. He was very sociable in that way, but he didn't do it to have an entourage follow him; he was generous because he wanted everyone else to enjoy everything.

He always had my back. I was friends with one of the neighborhood girls, and I spent the night at her house. As I was leaving the next morning, her next-door neighbor, an older woman who was watering her lawn in her bathrobe, recognized me and began calling me names and badmouthing my father, saying, "He thinks he's the king of everything!" I had never heard someone talk badly about him like that, and it affected me. When I got home, I told my dad what had happened, and he said, "Where does she live?" I told him, and he replied, "Let's go." We drove up to her house, and he got out and walked up to her, fully dressed in one of his outfits. I watched them converse for a few minutes, and by the end, she had asked him to sign a record for her, and they had taken a smiling picture together.

That's the type of father he was.

In the evening, if the vinyl doors were open, I'd hang out with him, but I'd get tired and go to bed, so he wouldn't tell me to go to bed very often. Graceland was very busy during the day, so that's when my father would sleep, but at night, it was peaceful for him because people would leave him alone.

However, hanging out with him could be a double-edged blade because I didn't want to quit whatever wicked behavior I was carrying out.

I had a friend—his girlfriend Ginger Alden's niece—who was a bit of a troublemaker. She was older than me, about eleven, and she had a motorcycle. That's freedom, I thought, and I want one.

But I got the impression that my father didn't want me on it. One day, while he was sleeping, Ginger's niece put me on the back of the bike. As we sped through a grassy area at Graceland, there was a laundry line across the lawn. Ginger's niece didn't see it and drove right through it—it got her around the neck and threw us both backward. The bike fell on my calf, and the muffler burned my leg badly.

I went to bed shortly after, and when I awoke in the middle of the night, he was standing next to my bed, holding a basset hound puppet and singing "Can't Help Falling in Love" to me.

Take my hand, and take my entire life.

For I can't help but fall in love with you.

When he finished singing, my dad hugged me and apologized.

Upstairs at Graceland is just how Elvis left it, so you can truly feel his presence.

We'd sometimes sleep in his bed, which my mother loved because it made her feel close to her father, and we felt the same way. However, because Elvis's bedroom isn't part of the tour and no visitors are permitted up there, if we woke up late and the tours had already begun, we'd be stuck in his room until late afternoon, when the tours would end. We'd have staff members bring us food, usually McDonald's, and just hang out all day.

During the tours, my mother enjoyed going through her father's books to better understand him. He was clearly looking for a deeper understanding of the world—most of the books were spiritual or self-help titles, such as Understanding Who You Are, Sacred Science of Numbers, and How to Be Happy, Kahlil Gibran's The Prophet, and even Ram Dass's Be Here Now--really human things. There were also lots of Bibles. Elvis would underline phrases and write thin" Next to them.

When you saw the undertones and the spiritual quest, you got a sense of the essentially broken feeling he shared with my mother; he was looking to mend himself, to find a deeper purpose, which she would also look for in her own life.

We'd often sit up there, and my mother would go line by line, really looking into everything he'd underlined, showing us, grasping at straws.

Then security would knock on the door and offer us sausage and biscuits, which we would consume.

You can still feel him in the room; his spirit is engraved there.

I vaguely recall a talk we had in that room regarding a section that Elvis had underlined; I began to contact someone to help me remember it, but realized there was no one there to call.

The fans were constantly out there, either resting on the fence or in the trees near the carport. There were forests and a chapel right next door. Creepers could just come in and sit on the side of the fence or in a tree outside the fence, where they would sit all day and night and watch. There were some monitors who had a monopoly on a certain tree—they'd come solely to watch my father move out of the home and into his automobile. We couldn't really do anything because it was church property. It was banned to enter the forests. My father would not allow it. It was completely out of the question.

I wasn't supposed to, so I drove my golf cart really quickly and near to the supporters, yelling obscenities at them. "Fuck you!" Fucker!" They'd simply sit there, smile, and wave.

Sometimes a fan would jump the fence, resulting in an all-points bulletin. Security would come to locate me and say, "Get in the house, somebody's gonna kill you!"

I took a fan's camera at one point, but I grew bored and didn't want to take pictures, so I chucked it into the bushes. I felt terrible after doing it more than once. My uncle Vester, who worked front gate security, would come up to the office and say, "Lisa has taken someone's camera again; should we try to find it?"

Years later, someone approached me and stated, "You took my camera when I was at the front gate and never came back!" I said, "Oh God, I'm so sorry."

I was Eloise in the Plaza.

I am not proud of it.

Every year, we went to Graceland for the annual Candlelight Vigil, which honors Elvis' death and attracts thousands of people from around the world.

I must have been around twenty years old that year, and I watched as an older admirer, clearly from Elvis' generation, hugged my mother. That fan was there every year, so I recognized her, but this time I was paying close attention to their connection; I was more aware of my mother's body language, perhaps because I was older. And the way my mother submitted into this woman's arms destroyed my heart. At that moment, I knew she was looking for a parent.

Going to his gigs was my absolute favorite thing in the world.

I was so proud of him. He would grab my hand and lead me out onstage, then walk me to his spot on the stage, and then take me away from him and lead me to my seat in the crowd. Usually with Vernon.

The electricity in such shows. Nothing I've ever felt compares to that feeling. Electrifying is a broad term, but it accurately describes how it felt. I loved seeing him perform. I enjoyed certain songs, such as "Hurt" and "How Great Thou Art." I would ask him to sing those songs for me, and he would always agree.

I did not, however, enjoy having the spotlight shine on me or being asked to stand in front of everyone. In Vegas, during his residency, he introduced Vernon and then glanced at me, and I remember thinking, Oh God, please don't. "Lisa, stand up!" It's not that I wasn't proud or loved him. I simply enjoyed the spotlight on him. It wasn't something that came to me naturally. I abhorred it.

But in other, less visible ways, I enjoyed reveling in his celebrity alongside him.

In Los Angeles, I attended John Thomas Dye School, located in the hills of Bel Air. I still pass past it occasionally to recall the day my father attended a parent-teacher meeting. I knew he was coming and couldn't wait. I could feel both the professors' fear and excitement. My young student mates were so excited that I became even more excited—everyone was running about like crazy.

Then my father showed up. He got out of the automobile wearing a respectable outfit--black slacks and some kind of blouse--but he was also wearing a large, majestic belt with buckles, gems, and chains, along with sunglasses. He was smoking a cigar. I met him in the car and walked up the path with him, and I still remember the sensation of walking next to him while holding his hand.

When I watch videos of Elvis performing, I sometimes think about how if he hadn't done exactly what he did at the right time--if he hadn't walked into the right building, recorded the right song, or danced the way he did in front of the right person--there would be no Elvis Presley. We'd probably have lived somewhere in Mississippi.

I haven't even finished high school in this version of my life, so I'm not sure where I'd be in that one. My great-grandfather drove trucks; perhaps we would have continued the tradition. Perhaps we could have produced furniture in Tupelo.

My mother would almost certainly have ended up in jail.

Yuki Koshimata was my nanny in California, where I lived with my mother. Yuki was a tiny Japanese woman who took excellent care of me. She was always there; she wrote to me until her death.

I received cards every Christmas and birthday, even after I married and had children.

I would wail whenever we dropped Yuki off at her house over the weekend or during her time off. I remember being in the car with my mother driving away and shouting at the top of my lungs as we drove out of sight of her.

I was quite attached to her.

Leaving Graceland and flying from Memphis International Airport back to Los Angeles was a tremendous emotional ordeal for me. But the moment I got out of the automobile in Memphis, I transformed entirely. I've never wanted to leave. I adored everything about it. I enjoyed the weather, the storms, the cold, the birdsong, and the firefly. I enjoyed the people and the scents. One of my favorite snapshot memories from when I was about seven or eight was getting off the plane in Memphis, gazing down, and seeing snow.

There were occasions when I was at school in Los Angeles and saw a black sedan turn up, and someone would come to the classroom to collect me so that I could go meet him. They'd get me on a plane and fly me to where he was. He would generally tell someone, "Go get her," and then whisk me away to wherever he was.

I waited for that automobile to arrive--it was always black, usually a Mercedes or a limousine. When that car came around, I felt like my life had never been better.

Sometimes he'd fly back with me. He would also land the fucking plane. At the end of the flight, he would take the copilot seat, making everyone uneasy, and say, "Ladies and gentlemen, please fasten your seatbelts, Elvis is going to land the plane."

I'd wonder, "Uh, can I get off?" I would tighten my seatbelt as far as it would go, and then I remember everyone celebrating when we landed because we were alive.

We were alive.

I was scheduled to return to Los Angeles because I was set to start school.

"Please, ask Mommy if she'll let me stay," I implored my father.

"I'll call her and ask her," he added, then told me to wait in my room. I remember pacing outside his door, in the hallway with the foot-long shag mat. Eventually, he emerged and hugged me. I heard this gasping sound. He was crying.

"You can't stay," he responded, because "she wants you to come home."

My father never spoke negatively about my mother. He didn't want me to think adversely about her. In retrospect, they did an excellent job of keeping a cohesive front and a genuine buddy bond. There was still a lot of affection between them, and they put up a nice front for me. I was quite lucky.

So he didn't want her to appear bad, but he was incredibly upset. He collected himself and continued, "You know, your mommy is correct. You have to return because you need to start school, and she needs to prepare you. I don't want you to leave, you know, but your mother is correct; it's the appropriate thing to do."

That gasping sound never left me, and he cried while trying not to show it. It demonstrated how much he loved me.

But I wasn't thrilled with my predicament. I remember picking up a book about Japan in school and thinking how beautiful everything was, the architecture, the ponds, and how much I wanted to live there. Not to seem ungrateful, but I was lonely in Los Angeles. I wasn't alone, yet I felt quite lonely. I didn't have many friends. So I would simply stare at the book, wishing I could live in the illustrations. So far away. Another world, another location, another time.

Music was the only thing that saved me. I had a little 45 record player, and music was the only thing that could transport me away. I would subsequently play Neil Diamond, Linda Ronstadt, and my father. I recall being in the center of my floor, with the record player in front of me.

That machine and my Snoopy doll were my imaginative companions. Snoopy was everything for me. I loved him so much that I stitched his nose back together. I had outfits for him, one for each day. He went with me everywhere. He was my best friend. I took him to school because I was frightened to be there, and they forced me to keep him in my locker, which I despised.

But knowing he was there helped me be more present.

My father's intensity was palpable at all times.

If the intensity was good, it was fantastic; if it was terrible, watch the fuck out. Take a step back. He had a magnetism about him. Whatever it was, it would be a thousand percent. When he became enraged, everyone ran, ducked, and took cover.

There was this one time—I believe it was during one of his trips in Tahoe. He always reserved the entire top floor of any hotel he was staying in for himself and his crew. That night, he was back in his bedroom, irate, yelling, and screaming. Someone instructed me to sit behind a chair in the main suite and not move. Everyone was attempting to hide behind something to get out of the fucking way. So I hid and saw him take things by the handful or harmful and throw them from the balcony. He had chosen his flight route and planned to fly it until he was finished hurling things off the balcony. He eventually calmed down, and someone told me, "It's okay, you can come out now, he wants to see you."

I thought, Does he want to see me?

"Why was he so mad?" I asked.

"Well," someone explained, "he ran out of water."

So I took four bottles of water and went into his room.

"Somebody told me you didn't have any water," I remarked, and he merely waved for me to come hug him.

He was respectful, though; he wasn't nasty to others, he wasn't angry, and he didn't dwell there. Some people live in complete destruction, while others acquire some real estate and walk around in rage for a short time. My father would just pay a visit.

My father would sometimes take me to Libertyland, a Memphis amusement park, and close it down for me and the rest of the group, as well as their families and friends. He and I would go on the roller coaster. I loved it.

One of my father's outbursts occurred when we were due to visit Libertyland. I'd invited all of my friends, but when I went upstairs the night before, I heard the wrong tone—a baritone sound with the wrong intensity. I went into my room and heard loud smashing sounds. He was screaming his fucking head off at someone. I could hear him announcing that we were not going to Libertyland the following day. I was devastated.

I learned later that he had run out of something again and needed to obtain it before we left--or they wouldn't give it to him. So he hit the roof and contacted ten different physicians and nurses before finding someone who could help him. He was alright after the nurse or doctor delivered the treatment he required. And we traveled to Liberty Land.

I remember sitting next to him on the Zippin Pippin roller coaster that day, one eye focused on the ride and the other on his gun in his holster, which was on my side. That sounds dreadful, unless you knew or understood him. You could think he was crazy for carrying a piece with his daughter sitting next to him, but he was simply from the South. It was simply so amusing.

We rode and rode.

That occurred roughly a week before his death.

Chapter 2: He's Gone

I was always afraid about my father dying.

Sometimes I'd see him, and he'd be out of it. Sometimes I found him passed out.

I wrote a poem containing the sentence, "I hope my daddy doesn't die."

He had a TV and a chair set up in my room, so he would frequently stop over and relax in the chair while smoking his cigars. I could wake up at any time and find him sitting there. I was once with a friend in my room, and when he approached my bedroom door, he began to collapse. I could tell he was leaning too far to the right, so I yelled, "Go get him!" My companion and I managed to crawl underneath him and hold him up until he grabbed something and regained his composure, at which point he simply returned to his room.

That happened several times: pleased to see me, followed by swaying.

And that happened frequently in the end.

I was sitting next to him in my room, watching television, and I said, "Daddy, please don't leave. "Please do not die."

He declared, "I'm not going anywhere."

He then grinned at me.

I knew something horrible was about to happen, which made me feel protective and like I needed to keep an eye out for him.

When I was strolling by his bedroom, he was resting flat on his back. I was scared when I noticed how large his stomach was.

Several days later, I was in my room with my pals. We were all in the hamburger bed, watching Brian's Song, a terrible movie. About halfway through the film, I became concerned about my father and went into his bathroom, where I discovered him face down. He'd held on to the towel rack, but it shattered and he fell. I dashed downstairs to get Delta; she called for assistance, and they got him up, gave him coffee, and got him going. I watched as they walked him around the room. He clung to them. His head was falling down at one point, but when he noticed me in the chair, we met gazes, and his entire face brightened up. He tried to get away from them and come over to where I was, but I could tell he was about to feel sick.

I answered, "No, he's going to throw up."

So they escorted him to the restroom, and sure enough, he became ill.

I did not say anything. I did not speak to anyone about anything. I just internalized everything.

My father wanted me to ride with him on a snowmobile one winter at Graceland, but I was terrified. He was a wildcard, a crazy man. But I went on the snowmobile nonetheless, since he was my father. He began descending the steepest stretch of the driveway. He lost control, and we began sliding and jumping the curb. We both hung on somehow and fell on the grass, laughing.

But there was another time when he and several of his fellow colleagues went down on sleds on their bellies, while the wives and kids stood about watching. I was at the top of the hill, terrified because there was no way to stop those sleds—no brakes, no ropes to pull on. I recall thinking, "Daddy, what are you doing?"

I saw my father fall on his stomach, and just like with the snowmobile, he leaped the curb at the bottom and rolled three times before lying there motionless. Everyone became agitated and began running toward him, fearing he had died. As they approached, terrified, he flopped over onto his back and let out a tremendous, guttural belly laugh like you wouldn't believe. He thought that was the funniest thing.

During the days, I ran around with a group of my relatives and friends. Sandy Miller was my grandfather's sweetheart; she lived across the field in the house with him. She had three children: two boys and one daughter. Laura was my age. She was one of my best friends. Deana Gambill, my cousin Patsy's daughter, was also my dearest friend. I was really protective of her and loved her a lot. But Laura and I would argue furiously. I would torture her and attempt to have her eat my makeup.

She and I were fighting in my room because I wanted her Barbie case, and she refused to give it to me.

"Give me that goddamn Barbie case," I snapped.

"No!"

"But I can't get it, nowhere has it, you better give it to me," I told you. Laura began screaming, "Nooooo!" when I grabbed up a statue in my room and held it over my head. Then she looked to my right, and I saw my father standing there. I quickly put down the statue and pretended we were just playing.

"What are you doing?" he asked.

"Nothing, just playing," I replied.

"Don't kill your best friend," he said. Words of wisdom.

When I was eight or nine years old, I had a great crush on one of Laura's brothers, Rory. I was head over heels, painfully in love with this boy for years. Rory stood five feet eleven, had dark hair, and was quite cute. He had a wonderful attitude, emerald eyes, and a beautiful smile. I couldn't move when he entered the room. He would promise to write me letters, and I would wait and wait. I'd tell Laura to ask Rory if he liked me. I would hold on to anything he said or did. Rory kissed me once or twice while we were playing hide-and-seek in the pool area downstairs, so I assumed it was mutual. I kept wanting to play hide and seek to see if he'd do it again.

He ended up with all these incredibly beautiful girls, and I was always so jealous--my God, I couldn't stand it. That would break my heart.

When I was about six or seven, I had spent the summer at Graceland, and my father had gone on tour, so my mother's mother arrived and took me up. We flew to New Jersey together to see her, my grandfather, and my mother's five other siblings in Mount Holly.

I never had a bond with my grandmother. When I was in the bathtub, she knelt over to rinse me, revealing her cleavage and a massive dark mole on her chest. I glanced at it and shouted screaming murder. "Don't you pick me up with that thing you've got right there!"

I had spent the summer with my father where there were no regulations, so I needed to be de-brat-icized, but I wasn't going for it. My mother's parents believed that I was nothing exceptional, that I would not be treated differently than the rest of their family. I used to scream my head off because the change was so perplexing. I recall shouting so loudly for an hour that my mother's younger brothers laughed at me.

My mother had my grandmother's frigid personality, which she inherited from her mother, my great-grandmother.

I once had a small cameo, a compact, and a scent that I adored. I couldn't find it one day, and I was so distraught and crying that everyone tried to help me find it. Then I recall sitting in the car and glancing down into my grandmother's pocketbook. There it was. I asked, "What's that?" She answered, "You didn't see anything, so it's nothing," and shifted her purse away.

I thought, Oh my God, the bitch took it from me!

I know I acted like a princess at times. But it's strange because I was/am full of self-doubt. It was all really confusing.

Looking back, I was certain of one thing: my father loved me.

We celebrated my ninth birthday in Lisa Marie, my father's plane. My father was in his bedroom in the back, but he came out to join everyone else in singing "Happy Birthday." Charlie Hodge, his onstage sidekick, approached me and emptied his pockets on the table, saying, "Take whatever you want." He didn't have a present, so I just grabbed the cash.

At the time, my father was dating Ginger Alden. He had a lot of different girlfriends, and I liked the majority of them. There was Sheila Caan and Linda Thompson, whom I adored. Linda clearly cared about me and my father. When they split up, he didn't tell me, so I hurried up to hug his girlfriend, thinking it was Linda, but it was Ginger. I didn't mind Ginger, but I didn't particularly like her. Nobody did.

She was usually really sweet to me, which was a no-brainer unless you were an idiot, but I didn't like how she upset him. I used to listen to their phone calls. He had one of those old phones where the line would light up and you could switch to another receiver. Those chats would drive me completely crazy. She was not there for him. I could tell she didn't love him at all. When he got into a quarrel with her, I remember the sound of his Stutz, his favorite automobile, screeching away. Because I knew they had been arguing, I was concerned when I heard him run off at high speed from the gate.

I remember him asking, "Have you seen Ginger?" Is she around?

"Where is she?"

"I don't know where she is," I said.

She was driving him crazy and playing him hard. She'd be there for him for a minute and then leave. One day, I went with her to see her relatives. I didn't tell him I was going, but I informed others, and she offered to take me, so I figured it was fine. When I returned, he was angry, which devastated me.

That relationship was extremely turbulent.

My mother learned from these experiences to prioritize her children over her relationships.

Anytime she got a new partner, she'd bring us into the kitchen and say, "Guys, this is [insert name]," then smile and watch as an awkward encounter occurred. But she always wanted to see our take on the new boyfriend; she trusted our senses.

Later, she'd ask, "What did you think, and did you like him?" If we answered no, he would leave. If he said something incorrect to us, she'd put him in his place.

Later that year, at the end of another incredible summer at Graceland, my father was preparing to go on tour. All of the large tour cases were lined up by the front door, ready for loading. He was leaving the next day, and I was heading back to California to begin school.

I was very depressed about leaving and didn't want to go.

My father had built a massive racquetball court, and my buddies and I had been spending late nights playing there. Very late, far after midnight. I was entering through the back door just as my father was exiting, and I ran into him.

He said, "Go to bed," and I agreed. I hugged and kissed him, and we both said "I love you." Then I went upstairs and slept.

I awoke abruptly in the early afternoon, and I sensed panic. Something didn't seem right. It seemed like a new kind of energy.

It wasn't uncommon for me to be awakened by a noise. One night, I was awakened by drilling, banging, singing, and other sounds. My father had wanted his organ moved upstairs so he could play and sing gospel in his room, but it wouldn't fit through his doors, so they had to do all of this construction to get it in.

I found Joe Esposito and asked, "What's going on with my father? Where is he?"

"Your daddy's sick," Joe remarked.

"What does that mean?" I exclaimed as I dashed into his bathroom, which was so large that it had a separate wash bucket for his hair. The shower was also massive, with a walk-in design that circled around. There was also a large closet with a bed inside for anyone who wanted to nap, I suppose. It had two entrances, one of which led directly into my room.

I ran across the restroom and there he was. Just as I was about to run to my father on the ground, someone grabbed me and pulled me back. They were standing over him, shifting him about and attempting to work on him. I screamed bloody murder.

I knew it wasn't good. Then I was hauled out of the room.

There were numerous occasions when I discovered him on the floor or unable to control his body. It was barbiturates.

They gripped me and led me downstairs. A stretcher was taken upstairs. I was inside the dining room. The entrance door was wide-open. They pushed the stretcher down the steps, right past me. I couldn't see his face, but I did see his head, body, pajamas, and socks at the bottom of the gurney.

I broke free from whoever was holding me and went for the stretcher. Someone pulled me back. They needed to keep working on him.

It was lightning fast.

He had not been proclaimed dead yet. They pulled him away, and I began shouting that I wanted him, that I needed him, and I began kicking and beating whoever was holding me back, attempting to flee, but they would not let me go.

The front door closed.

To be fair, if I had gotten to him, I would have seen his disfigured face, which would have further horrified me.

Then we only had to wait. I kept saying, "Is he going to be okay, is he going to be okay?"

Someone was saying: "We're just waiting for the hospital to call us to tell us."

I grabbed my buddy Amber, Ginger's niece, and we headed upstairs to my room. While we waited, I lit a cigarette and sprayed Windex in the air, thinking no one would smell it.

Ginger had somehow found time to do her hair and cosmetics. She was dressed to the nines.

It had been almost an hour since I heard my grandfather sobbing and wailing. That noise. I'll never get over the sound of him sobbing. I couldn't understand what he was saying, so I went downstairs.

As I approached, I could hear, "Ohhhhh, ohhhhh, he's gone, he's gone." Everyone was in the room, including my grandfather, Ginger, Aunt Delta, and my great-grandmother.

Everyone but my father.

"Who's gone?" I asked.

"Your papa has left! "My son is gone," my grandfather exclaimed.

I was furious. I went crimson red, turned around, and began to flee. Ginger tried to grab the back of my shirt to keep me still, but I just fucking fled. I'm not even sure where I ran. I think I ran upstairs, back to my room, and locked the door. I can't recall what I did after that.

I just wasn't sure what to do. My initial reaction was rage, tremendous fury, followed by grief. I'm not sure why, but I was angry at the cosmos for allowing this to happen. I drove out in my golf cart, toward one of the trailers in the back. We were watching the news, and it hit me hard.

My life as I knew it was finished.

It's your greatest childhood fear: you don't want to lose the person you love. It's fucking terrifying and tortures you. That is something that most children worry about. When I told my father that I was afraid he was going to die, he said, "I'm not going anywhere, I'm not going anywhere."

But he did.

Later, I was heading down the stairs of the house and noticed the tour cases. It appeared that he was about to come down the stairs and take them on a tour. Then I recall thinking, "Am I going to be able to return to Memphis?"

That afternoon, after they took him away—which is something I've been unhappy about my entire life—it became a free-for-all. Everyone went to town. Before he was proclaimed dead, everything was taken and wiped clean, including jewelry, antiquities, and personal items.

Things from that day are still coming up for auction.

I heard my mother was on her way to me. It was the worst. It seemed like an invasion—Graceland was my home with my father, and I didn't want her there. She was going to ruin the whole vibe. I had friends and folks around. Not only was she going to take me home, which I didn't enjoy, but she was also coming to the funeral.

Then I had another notion of not being able to return here anymore. My grandfather was still living, so I had an excuse to visit.

But would she allow me?

She finally arrived, and I was riding in a golf cart with a friend or two. I recall her standing in the doorway at the front steps of Graceland, yelling my name and attempting to wave me down. I simply returned the gesture and continued on my way. She shrieked at me: "How can you be on a golf cart right now?" I refused to pay her any attention since I was so unhappy.

I didn't understand why I was yelled at, but now I see she was probably thinking about the fans on the street. They could see me, and she presumably thought it was terrible publicity for me to be going around on a golf cart with my pals after my father had died.

Because the entire world had halted.

The screening was intended to be a public event. My father was brought to the house. They held him in the living room, which is the chamber before the piano room on the right as you enter the front entrance. I was ecstatic that he was there. I felt fortunate.

I waited on the stairs leading upstairs with a couple of my friends and witnessed unending oceans of people passing through the line, fainting, yelling, crying, and grieving so deeply. I'm not sure whether anyone noticed me; they might have, but they were too focused on him.

For numerous hours, I sat and watched.

Every hour, ambulances arrived outside to transport persons who had fainted. It felt as if the entire country was there. You couldn't even see the streets because there were so many people.

I was so preoccupied with everyone else's pain that I couldn't experience mine yet. I was trying to grieve for my father, but I also recognized him as "Elvis Presley." I knew his persona and that he enjoyed being Elvis the best.

Watching other people weep about my father made me decide not to grieve publicly. I simply didn't. I could not.

I'm not sure how long the watching lasted, but there was a lot of drama. I held it all in. I'd say, "Wow, look at that person; they're completely losing it." Then I would go grieve in my room, where no one could see me, or at night before going to bed.

I wasn't sure what to do with my grief. I would do things to occupy myself, which worked for a short time, but if I had a minute, I would lose it.

I went down to where he was resting in the casket simply to be with him, to touch his face, hold his hand, and talk to him. I asked him, "Why is this happening? "Why are you doing this?"

I knew he would soon be gone. I can't recall much after that. I was nine. Everything was so fucking beyond me.

It will continue to hammer me, on and off. As an adult, I used to get drunk, listen to his music, and sit there crying.

The grief continues to come.

It is still just there.

My life changed dramatically after my father died. Beyond my grandparents, I kept in touch with Patsy and one or two Memphis Mafia members, such as Jerry Schilling. The rest sort of slipped away.

My mother remained in Memphis until everything was settled, and in October, my father was relocated from Forest Hill Cemetery to the backyard of Graceland, next to his mother. That was the first time I truly felt a sense of loss, not just from my father's death, but also from the fact that I felt stuck with this lady. It was a one-two punch: he died, and I'm now trapped with her.

My mother took me to Europe with her sister. Rome, France, and London. She attempted to keep me very occupied.

They escorted me to Buckingham Palace. The journalists went bananas. They kept finding us no matter where we went. But at the palace, it was a peaceful day. I observed the changing of the guard. I was annoyed. I wondered, what are we doing out here? Why aren't we going inside? Why are we standing out here trying to get in when people can simply enter Graceland? I didn't get it.

One night in France, I told my mother that I was the reborn Marie Antoinette and that I needed to go to Versailles. So she took me there, and I was wandering around saying, "Yeah, I recognize this, I recognize that...."

Prior to going to Europe, I spent six weeks at Rancho Oso, a summer camp in the highlands north of Santa Barbara.

At camp, I had a horse that I adored and rode frequently. That was healing. Then I'd be at the pool, having fun with the kids, and then suddenly feel unwell. I'd become preoccupied for a minute and then say, "Oh my God, my father died." I was lying in the sun when an Elvis song played on the radio, and I simply cried for an hour.

Most of those kids had no idea who I was, and I didn't want to tell them, but then several of them began bragging to me about having attended Elvis Presley's funeral in Memphis.

"I saw his dead body," someone added.

"No, you didn't," I replied.

"Yeah, we were there...."

"I'm his daughter," I explained. "You were not there. I was there. "I understand."

After camp, my mother wanted me to attend a decent school, so she enrolled me in a prestigious one in Los Angeles. Everyone had a renowned father and mother, but I wasn't interested.

Then my mother found a French partner and became fascinated with being French, so she enrolled me in a French school and made me take fucking French classes.

I desired to reclaim my previous existence.

I've always wanted to go to Memphis. I wanted to make sure I could go to Memphis, and that's what mother used to threaten me with: "You're not going to be able to go to Memphis if you don't blah, blah, blah..." It irritated me, but I'd do whatever it took. She knew that was everything to me.

I kept my watch set to Memphis time.

She let me go every Christmas, Easter, and summer. I would stay with Patsy, who was like a mother figure to me, and spend time with her and her children. It meant a lot to be part of that family.

Every Sunday was cleaning day, and we'd watch movies, eat biscuits and gravy and sausage, drink large bottles of Pepsi, go to the video store, or spend the night at Graceland. My aunt continued to reside there for several years after my father died. I'd go sleep over there while she was still alive. The kitchen wasn't yet accessible to the public, so I'd stay in the room just off of it.

Upstairs was locked. I could go up there, but I needed to come back down. I'm not sure why, maybe because his room was there. I believe there were many discussions about what to do with the upstairs to keep it maintained, but Vernon and my mother agreed I couldn't go back into my room.

Vernon died in 1979, and a year later, my great-grandmother died. I recall a car pulling up to school on both occasions. It became customary for an automobile to appear unexpectedly. I grew used to it. I started thinking, "There's the car; who is it now?"

I had no emotional connection with my granddad. He had a harsh demeanor. I never moved past that with him.

When we were alone, my friend and I started toying with my grandfather's face in his casket. That's not something I want to express lightly because I know how horrible it is. There were stitches on him—I had no idea why, but I suppose they had to open him up and let the corpse drain.

I was growing numb to everything. Just another funeral and another loss. Memphis was becoming a place where people only returned for funerals. I'd been through enough trauma that it no longer affected me. Everyone expected me to be upset, yet nothing bothered me. There was simply so much trauma.

Sometimes I'd walk into my mother's room and find her sitting alone on the floor, intoxicated, listening to her father's music and crying. But she'd never discuss it or listen to his songs when sober.

It's tough to go about your day without hearing an Elvis song, but I recall the first time my mother played Elvis in the vehicle. Of course, there were instances when his songs would come on at a café or she'd come across them while changing the radio channel, and I'd find her leaving them on. But one day, when my sisters were young, we were all driving somewhere, and I realized it was the first time she had chosen to listen to Elvis Radio on Sirius while driving. She informed my sisters, "This is your grandfather." I recall thinking it was both bizarre and sweet.

I was twenty-two.

I don't believe she ever processed the loss. I believe she began using phrases like trauma in the last year of her life--as late as 2021. But I knew she was heartbroken all my life. I remember being angry at Elvis as a child for abandoning my mother and creating so much sorrow.

Every time I heard Elvis' voice, I felt my mother's sorrow. Feel the loss of him.

My granddad had known I had a thing on Rory Miller.

After Vernon died, I learned that the Millers were relocating to Colorado. I was scheduled to meet and hang out with Rory before they departed; in fact, I had planned to spend the entire day with him. Patsy knew, and at the last minute, I received a phone call: "Your mother wants you to fly home to Los Angeles today." Patsy had told my mother, and she was not having it.

I was devastated. Rory transported me to the airport. That was the first time I recall having genuine, specific hatred for my mother.

I saw Rory many years later when on tour, and we had dinner with him, his wife, and Patsy. According to Rory, "Your father pulled me aside and told me, you better not do anything, or I'll fucking kill you." My father didn't use the F-word carelessly, so the message was heard clearly. Rory claimed he promised my father he would never do anything romantic with me, and he also vowed not to tell me about the talk.

"But I think I can probably say it safely now," Rory admitted.

My mother sent me away frequently, but I must add that she was particularly good at birthdays.

One year, I remember seeing the Queen at the Forum. I'd heard that Freddie Mercury was a big fan of my father, so I gave him one of his scarves. I watched the show and then went backstage to meet Freddie, who was quite nice, humble, and moved by the gift.

When I was ten years old, my mother contacted John Travolta and arranged for him to meet me on my birthday. He was having a hot moment with Welcome Back, Kotter. He told her about Scientology, and a few days later, she joined. I was in the car with her, and she was telling me how it can make you annoyed. I remember wanting to spend the night at Catya's house because all of my friends had been able to stay there, plus she had an elevator! I was really excited to go, but my mother wouldn't let me. She believed Catya was spoiled and did not want me to be near her. My mother then became friends with Vidal and Beverly Sassoon, and Catya died from a drug overdose at the age of thirty-three.

I can tell that my mother was powerful in a positive sense; she was most concerned about me being spoiled. I don't think I was--I think I was absent-minded about stuff, but I don't think I was intentionally pampered. I know my father spoiled me, but my mother did the reverse.

My mother was really strict. She was never a friend or someone I could talk to.

I felt as if I were her trophy. She requested a cotillion for me. I had no idea what that was, but she always wanted one. She urged me to finish school. I thought she should have gotten a different daughter. It was about how things looked--the appearance seemed to be more significant than the sentiments. My mother would never allow herself to lose control. Everything was in its place.

My mother was gone a lot. She was either on an island eating something she caught in the ocean, in another strange location, or on another adventure with another man, so I started hiring more nannies and cooks. She employed a lot of individuals, and I became close to several of them.

My aunt and uncle, Michelle and Gary, who lived in our house, made me feel the most secure. At the time, we had a long corridor with my room near the end and Michelle and Gary's room all the way at the other end. That hallway terrified me at night, but when they were present, I felt better.

Michelle and Gary were the only people I could actually talk to.

When my mother was away, I could invite a buddy over; that was always my saving grace. But I had a difficult time making friends. I still don't. Maybe they thought I was a spoiled brat when I was actually afraid. I attended a prestigious school with celebrity students who speak French, travel the world, and work tirelessly to excel.

I wasn't into any of that. I felt quite insecure, apprehensive, and scared. People wouldn't make friends with me because they'd become competitive over who had the wealthier parents and the larger house.

It still happens. People say I'm a bitch because I have my mother's chilly thing.

I was slipping behind in all subjects. I'd shut myself in my room and listen to my records-music constantly.

Twice a year following his death, I would have dreams about my father. The dreams were so real that I would cry when I woke up because I felt like I was with him and didn't want them to end. I'd try so hard to fall back asleep and be with him again.

I don't really think they were dreams. I suppose these were visits.

I know many people will disagree with me and call that foolishness. You may have similar dreams and dismiss them as unimportant. That is OK. But I believe that those we love from our past can pay us a visit.

That was something my father would do on a regular basis.

In my dreams, he and I were together in my room. I am on my hamburger bed, and he is in the recliner. We're close and talking. Suddenly, I panic and say, "Wait!" You must stop this, Daddy! You need to wait! You're going to overdose and suffer a heart attack. Daddy! You are about to die. "It will happen."

And in the dream, my father looks at me calmly, knowingly, and grins, saying, "Darlin', it's already happened."

And then I would awaken.

My son was born in 1992, and the dreams came to an end there.

Chapter 3: The Wall

When I was about 10 years old, my mother sent me to many different schools in Los Angeles. One was in Los Feliz, while another was in Culver City. Our housekeeper, a lovely Black lady named Ruby, would drive me to school in the morning and play gospel music, which was all I wanted to hear because that was what my father had listened to.

The schools were very casual--no uniforms, not rigorous like the prior, more upscale institutions I'd attended--and I found them refreshing. I performed well there since I could learn at my own pace. I could merely finish an assignment and check it off as done. I didn't need to do anything remarkable there, either. I felt absolutely no pressure. I don't do well in groups, whether at job, school, or otherwise, so individualized learning appealed to me. The other kids were also quite unassuming and typical; there were no cliques, affluent kids, spoiled kids, bullies, or bitches.

However, during the next few years, I began to develop a negative mindset and became deeply involved in drugs. They booted me out of the Culver City school. Scientology didn't want to completely expel me, so they put me to the Apple Scientology school in Los Feliz. They expected this new school to be more capable of handling me, but I failed everything every single time.

I didn't mean to be bad. I honestly did not give a fuck. I wore all black and dyed my hair black. I had a "fuck you, fuck authority, fuck any system, fuck teachers, fuck parents" mentality. It was during this time that I found Pink Floyd's album The Wall. That record became everything I listened to and was interested in. It was both my bible and autobiography.

We don't need any schooling...

I was always in the ethics office, which was basically the principal's office. (I can't tell you how many people I've met since then who say, "I met you in ethics...." I joined that school on probation and never left. I kept missing either PE, which I never liked, or school altogether.

My mother struggled to keep me under control. There was nothing she could do. It wasn't easy for her. You could not torment me into wanting to learn. I wasn't interested in becoming a good kid. So one Friday, my mother picked me up from school and drove us up to Montecito, where she had a house, and as soon as we arrived, she said, "Pack your clothes, you're going to school in Ojai."

I knew by then that she was considering enrolling me in a boarding school in Switzerland or on a kibbutz in Israel; I had found four or five applications to various institutions. I felt like my mother was constantly trying to figure out how to send me away; aside from Switzerland and Israel, she had largely just thrown me into Scientology because she thought they could manage me. Scientology basically raised me for her. But every time mother tried to get me into a boarding school, I messed up the admissions test, and they wouldn't accept me.

But now I was on my way to board at Happy Valley School in Ojai, and I was mortified. The school was plainly intended for parents who just wished to send their children away. Some wanted to earn a decent education, but others wanted to do so simply because.

I was there "just because."

When I arrived, the first thing I did was look for anyone with weed. I quickly realized that the majority of the students shared my interests and were as energetic as I was, so I began to like it. We were out in the countryside with nothing to do.

I would spend the weekends with my mother in Montecito, which was only an hour away--unless I was on campus, which meant I had gotten into trouble during the week and couldn't go home. And I kept getting into problems, so my probation was prolonged. I used to skip class, despite the fact that we all slept approximately a hundred feet away from the classrooms. Sometimes there was a drug bust, and they'd look into who was involved, even though it was always me.

I was constantly falling behind in my schoolwork and performing poorly. I had been lousy at arithmetic from birth, and I had no interest in pursuing a job or even a topic. I had no desire to be a nice kid, either.

As I already stated, I honestly did not give a crap.

I began to go through various phases. At one time in Ojai, I was a hippy chick, a punk rock chick, and a funk rock youngster. I only wanted to do drugs, specifically cannabis and cocaine. I wasn't addicted to a certain chemical. I enjoyed everything. I wanted to get my hands on whatever I could swallow, snort, consume, or sniff. I never encountered heroin, however. I was never in the same room with it, thank God. (It would happen later.) My major goal in life was simply to find a score. I quickly fell into a heavy metal phase, dyeing my hair completely black or bleaching it, and using drugs.

But Happy Valley didn't want to throw me out because they were aware of my difficult home situation.

Every summer, the head of the Apple School would take a group of kids to Spain, where she had a house, and although I was no longer a student there, my mother insisted that I go. The five of us kids would take care of the property—gardening, farming—and then have fun at night by going to the beach and partying.

I managed to make it through my first year in Ojai.

When I was younger, my mother would take us to Ojai whenever possible so that we could ride horses in the valley. She had a special connection to the Ojai Valley from her school days, and she had always liked horses, understood how to treat them, cursed at them, and was never violent around them. I was just depressed, sullen, and dark. I am sure she didn't know what to do with that.

When I returned from Spain, I didn't want to go back to Ojai, but I had no choice. I skipped the first week, and when I returned, a new wild girl had arrived. She'd been waiting for me and began following me around. She said, "I've heard a lot about you..." She appeared cool and fascinating, but I was having a relationship with this German kid at the time, so when she had sex with him, I realized I was done being up here. So I claimed I was high on drugs to my mother.

"Mom," I whispered with regret, "if I stay up here I'm going to die."

She did indeed take me out of Happy Valley.

My mother had been dating a man named Michael Edwards. They dated for around six years in all.

Edwards was an actress and model, a dramatic individual with a terrible temper. He was also a frequent drug user. He and my mother would continuously quarrel, and it was physical. I would hear her scream.

They would party hard, go to discos, and there was a lot of cocaine around. When they returned home following a night out, I could hear him shouting and the furniture flying. It was quite destabilizing.

In the strangest turn of events, Edwards landed a role in the film Mommie Dearest, playing Joan Crawford's lover. One day, while he was still working on the film, my mother came into my room, searched through my wardrobe, and yelled at me because I was using wire hangers. These are from the cleaners! These should be switched with the beautiful ones, the plastic ones!"

We could hear laughs down the hall while she was ranting.

"The irony!" Michael shouted. "This is so crazy that you're actually yelling at your daughter about wire hangers and I'm in Mommie Dearest!"

My mother recognized the absurdity of the situation and began laughing as well. I thought, "This is my life now." You're both nuts.

My mother planned to re-enroll me in the Apple School, but because I was so far behind in my studies, they advised her that I would require daily tutoring, so I stayed at my mother's house with Edwards. But I didn't want to be there either. I didn't really want to be anywhere. I'm not sure what I wanted.

I probably just wanted my father.

I was continually displaying attitude and blasted hard metal on my record player all day.

My mother made dinner one night, and when I cut into the chicken, I discovered it was undercooked, so I informed her. The next thing I knew, Edwards overturned his plate, sending it flying across the room and smashing into the wall. I flung my palms up as if to exclaim, "What the fuck?" At that, he leaped up, began screaming gibberish, and bolted from the room.

When he returned, he was holding the end of the cord that connected to my record player—he'd cut it off with scissors. He continued ranting.

"Your mother cooks and you just blast your fucking rock and roll, your fucking music, your rock and roll music...." He wasn't making any sense. He eventually called for me to get out. I was shocked. As I exited the kitchen, I could hear them begin to speak about me, attempting to figure out what to do with me.

I went seeking cocaine. I had some concealed somewhere, but I couldn't recall where it was.

Edwards first came into my room in the middle of the night, intoxicated and kneeling, years ago. I believe I was ten. I awoke to find him on his knees next to my bed, running his finger up my leg beneath the sheets, and if I moved, he stopped--so I did. I was awake, but I tried to fall asleep.

He said he was going to teach me what would happen when I grew up. He was putting his hand on my chest and saying, "A man will touch you here," and then he put his hand between my legs and said, "They will touch you here." I believe he gently kissed me and then left that night.

I informed my mother the next day in the car, as I saw her slam the throttle pedal. At home, I dashed to my room, and she slammed the door shut.

She eventually called me in and explained that Edwards wanted to apologize.

Edwards was sitting on their bed, looking morose and depressed. He went on: "I'm so sorry, but in Europe that's how they teach the kids, so that's what I was doing."

I wasn't sure what to say. I always felt sorry for him when he apologized.

Eventually, he started touching and spanking me, telling me not to stare.-"Don't look at me," he'll say, or "don't turn your head." I believe he was jerking off. He wouldn't get angry with me since he did it quietly, sitting in a chair and whacking my ass. My buttocks would be black, blue, orange, and green.

It was pretty much the same drill every time. He'd enter the room and do what he did. I once showed my mother my buttocks, and she asked, "Well, what did you do to cause that?" as if he had just spanked me for misbehaving. And then she would shout at him. He'd state, "Oh, I was drunk," or worse, "She was actually flirting with me." Then she'd have him come in and apologize. I'd feel horrible and forgive him.

I was eleven, twelve, and thirteen.

He'd still come into my room every now and then, but I'd move or do something to make him think I was waking up, and he'd race down the hallway back to my mother's room, stress out, and leave.

My mother was attempting to establish a career at this stage in her life. She was striving to be a model and actor, as well as performing commercials, so she spent a lot of time away from town. And, as odd as that sounds, Edwards was more present than my mother. I was more accustomed to having him around than her.

Every Christmas, my mom would give me great things, but he didn't have much money to do the same. I used to cry on Christmas Day because I felt horrible for him. He was really severe on himself, and he played the role of a miserable victim.

But he still had a bad temper. He made a statement one morning about how I needed to grab my panties out of the dryer. I believe I mumbled something horrible back, like, "It's not like you're not enjoying that...." under my breath as I walked out of the room. He grabbed a dining room chair and flung it at me. It smacked me in the back—not hard, but enough to terrify the snot out of me. I cried the entire way to school.

I was crying all morning, and one of the teachers I really loved noticed me crying and asked what had happened. She pulled me aside and said, "You needed to break down and lose it!" because I was such a tough guy most of the time.

There was a great deal of fighting in the house. I would hear my mother scream and wail, and he would be hurling shit. I wanted to protect her. I didn't know how.

It was particularly awful during one of his modeling business travels to the Virgin Islands. My mother and I went with him. My mother feared he was having an affair with one of the models, so she asked me to help her catch him. My mother went into his room, and I could hear them arguing. I went in and watched him grab her and throw her into the bed. I jumped across the room and landed on his back, and he flung me onto the bed as well. My mother exclaimed, "Let's go, let's go!" We rushed down the hall, reached an elevator, and pressed the button, and he chased us while we frantically waited for the elevator door to open, like a scene from a horror film. We got it back to my room, and he called her - he'd reverted back into a puppy dog, asking her to return to him.

I was furious when she did this.

The next day, I departed for Memphis, but I was a complete wreck.

Hearing my mother narrate these events crushed my heart. I understand what happened was one of her worst childhood traumas, but I don't think she--or any of us who knew her--considered how that might have led to some of the underlying feelings she retained, such as guilt and self-hatred.

I turned fourteen, and my first relationship was with a schoolmate. Initially, we were really harsh to one other; my friends would think it was because he had a crush on me, and I would pursue him as well. But when we returned to school after the summer, he had transformed into a lovely young man with a lower voice; he was no longer the little chubby obnoxious prick. So we dated for a year, did everything but have sex. He was a nice child, but he had a bad temper.

My mother was in the Bahamas for an acting job in a movie of the week with Michael Landon. I went to see her, and there was a twenty-three-year-old guy who had a little role in the film as well. I didn't meet him until the day before my departure, and I fell hard. We went along the beach, conversing the entire time, and he was quite cute. I sat with him as he packed. I was very sad, but then he kissed me and we left the islands. I recall listening to the song "Torn Between Two Lovers" on the airplane ride home over and over again because I still had my boyfriend in Los Angeles, whom I had been dating for a year.

When I came home, I broke up with him.

I used to phone the twenty-three-year-old and remain silent. So he got used to the quiet caller. He didn't recognize me because there was no caller ID at the time. The first time he said, "Hello, who is this, hello, hello?" I was annoyed. Next time, he said, "It's you again." Finally, I started entering digits to answer yes or no to his inquiries. "Have we met?" Beep. "Do we know each other?" Boop. Then he figured it out. I was very nervous.

The guy was naturally nervous about seeing me, and I had no idea how I was going to meet up with him. One day at school, I informed my teachers that I needed to go to the dentist, and he drove me a few blocks away.

We walked around Beverly Hills all day. I didn't care what we were doing, where we were, or anything. I simply wanted to be with him.

He handed me his ring at the end of it. Then he dropped me off just before I was supposed to return to school.

I was gone. Really, truly gone.

My mother found out, and I was grounded, barred from speaking to or contacting him, which obviously didn't work. Not that I wouldn't have done the same thing if I were her, believe me, but I wasn't going to back down. I was utterly and madly in love.

After that, he was always creeping around. My mother told me I could see him, but we weren't permitted to be alone. We'd have to go somewhere my mother knew about and could see. He could come over and hang around, or I could invite him to go somewhere where my mother was also going, and he became friends with Edwards, of course. He was twenty-three years old and was being chaperoned by someone's mother. However, history repeated itself. My mother was fourteen when she met my father. I was recreating her life in an odd sense, but she and my father waited until she was eighteen to have sex. I was fourteen when I lost my virginity to this guy.

When I saw him, I just wanted to have sex or make out. This is all I could think of. We'd find somewhere to go or sit in his car in a parking lot. I'd tell my mother that I'd meet her somewhere and that we'd go for a walk before finding somewhere to make out.

But he was a complete womanizer. He had been with everybody. He was that guy from high school, that guy on the set. Women of all ages fell in love with this motherfucker. And it was so simple for him to maintain his normal life, with his other ladies, because I couldn't see him very often, and even when I did, it was only for a short period.

When I eventually met folks who knew him or went to school with him, they told me about a van he had that girls would use during breaks, lunch, and recess. He was a complete and whole player.

Even more, every woman fell in love with him. It was wild. My mother knew a woman who was a Playboy bunny back then. When I began dating this guy, the Playboy bunny was already having an affair with him, and my mother informed me that this woman was attempting to persuade my mother to send me to that kibbutz in Israel to get me out of the way.

I was with him for two and a half years.

The finale was simply a nightmare.

He took me to a park and had his friend discreetly photograph us. They sold the story and were compensated for the photographs. He did not care about me. It was just an opportunity for him. Our connection was unlawful, and selling those images exposed him, but the media at the time didn't care that I was young and simply published this personal information.

I had no idea he had scheduled the photo session. He later disputed it, but my mother informed me it was him.

When I found out, I took twenty Valium and made sure that someone saw me. I wasn't very serious about my suicide attempt. I went to the local hospital, and they gave me ipecac to make me vomit, which was the end of it. But I was truly crushed. That was my first great love and betrayal.

I was not going to be happy until I got my retribution. My mother came up with an idea. She didn't want to tell me the facts because I was still chatting to the guy occasionally. But, I believe, he was dealing blows, so it was planned that some off-duty cops would do a drug bust. She planned to embarrass him in the process.

She informed me they performed an anal probe.

When my mother first told me about this betrayal, she claimed it was her first recollection of feeling exploited, the first time she recognized others had an agenda for her. She talked about it throughout her life; it was a major trauma for her. It was only one of a sequence of experiences from her youth that contributed to her developing a fear of people—a suspicion she never fully recovered from.

I went back to school, but as soon as they put an algebra book in front of me, I left. I wasn't sure why I was there in the first place. Nobody asked what I was interested in. If you're going to put a child in school for so many years, you should at least find out what they're interested in. No one ever explained why I was even in school.

I remember reading my report cards as a child, and all they ever said was that I was really exhausted and loathed PE. And I felt dejected.

Actually, everyone who saw me after I was nine, when my father died, claimed I looked so melancholy.

My mom forced me to live with her again, but I was miserable and a terror. It was evident she did not want me there. She tried to force me to attend other boarding schools, but it didn't work, so she made me pack my bags and drove me to the Scientology Celebrity Centre, where she dropped me off.

The woman who operated the property led me to a little room on the third level. I was just happy to be out of my mother's place.

The first morning, I took the enormous mirror off the wall, contacted my coke dealer, and invited him and perhaps six or seven others over. We ended up having a four-day bender in the room.

I awoke at one point, and everyone was sleeping. I had a moment when I was completely done. I made a scene: "Everyone wake up, get the fuck out, out, get out!" I took the remainder of the blow and flushed it down the toilet.

I went down to where they audit people, and I started shivering, sweating, and crying. "Help me," I murmured, scarcely able to speak.

They relocated me to a pretty lovely room on the sixth story, which was like a luxury palace with a kitchen, dining room, and everything. They made me pledge to behave myself, study, produce, and truly do stuff. For whatever reason, it worked. For the next few months, I actually did very well. My mother then attempted to force me to return to her home. And that is when fucking DEFCON 3 began.

It was Christmas.

For whatever reason, I had to accompany her and Edwards to Pensacola, Florida, where his daughter lived. She and I were supposed to stay at home, and we pretended to, but we ended up going out. We didn't use drugs, and I believe we tried to drink, but the point was that I lied. My mother and Edwards showed up at her place. When I saw my mother step out of the car, I took off running down the street, my mother after me.

I'm flying; my mother is shouting at me, but she can't grab me. In the end, I got into her car—she's in the front seat, I'm in the back, and she's yelling at me because I'm avoiding her efforts to strike me. Edwards was attempting to get her off of me. I'm punching myself in the face, trying to make it look dramatic so it appears she did it.

The next day, we went back to Los Angeles, and she would not allow me to leave her sight. During the delay, I was desperate to get to a phone and call the Celebrity Centre for assistance. But my mother wouldn't even let me go to the bathroom without her.

Back in L.A., my mother was bringing me into the lobby of the Celebrity Centre to retrieve some of my belongings from my room, and it felt like someone was holding a pistol to my back. As we proceeded, I noticed a person I'd never forget--he had a black leather jacket, boxers, and black boots--and my eyes grew wide, and I tried to mouth, "Help me."

My mother drove me home that night, and intense negotiations began the next day. She agreed to allow me return to the Celebrity Centre, but only if I went to their Narconon office and entered their rehabilitation program.

"Give me a minute," I said. I called a friend's father and asked him what to do. He instructed me to ask for 24 hours to think about it, which I did, and the next day, I informed the rehab that I appeared to have three options: live with my mother and Edwards, go to Narconon, or hit the streets.

I told them I had chosen the third alternative.

"Hold on, hold on!" they exclaimed. The negotiations resumed this time at a nearby Jack in the Box—and I told them I wanted to live back in the room I'd had there, with my freedom, and that I'd do whatever I wanted—reading, studying—but that all I cared about was living at the Celebrity Centre in my room. They eventually reached an agreement.

So, I went. I soon found myself knocked out intoxicated in front of my room.

And then they came up with a fantastic concept. They forced me to care for someone who came in with a true drug addiction. They provided me a car so I could drive her around and aid her with her daily life. I became quite close to that girl and took her under my wing. She was a young mother who had been addicted to heroin. Her husband and kids had no idea. I genuinely enjoyed caring for her and helping others.

So now I have my own apartment in the Celebrity Centre and have made many acquaintances there. And I'd occasionally link up with the older man who sold the images of me. I recall he was living with a woman--I'm not sure if he married her--but one afternoon I met him at their house and we had sex while she was gone.

The guy wanted to meet up with me more and establish a relationship with me, but I had already met and fallen in love with a guy named Danny Keough.

Chapter 4: There's A Bluebird In My Heart

I'd heard a lot about Danny Keough.

He was twenty-one years old when we met, and I had just turned seventeen. He was in Los Angeles from Oregon and was the bass player in a band called D'bat, which played modest gigs around town. They were all quite cute and popular, and the females were particularly fond of Danny. They were also in love with the lead vocalist, a man named Alex, but he was not as cool or rough as Danny, and he liked himself. A lot. We used to tease Alex because he was always checking his own reflection on the back of spoons.

I later learned that all of the males in D'bat had crushes on me, but I wasn't paying attention. I've always been quite foolish about such things. I don't make assumptions, and I had little self-confidence back then. And the moment I heard someone was a heartbreaker, a ladies' guy, or a womanizer, I raised my guard. I was already guarded, but I'd add another layer if I thought someone was an asshole, especially after what occurred with the older boyfriend who sold the images. I had those protections, but I could also be extremely stupid, like a schoolgirl.

I was still living at the Celebrity Centre, but I was also returning to live with my mother. I had a birthday celebration for myself at the rose garden café in the back of the center, and it was the first time I was in the same room as Danny. Our initial interaction was a quick drive-by, and I forgot about it. About a week later, I had completely moved back into my mother's house, and everyone from the rose garden party was going to supper at the Mustache Café on Melrose. Danny was there, and he was making these remarks that bothered me—I thought he was arrogant and overconfident. I'd react, and I could see he was annoyed. That night, we all ended up at a party in the Hollywood Hills, and when the birthday cake came out in front of everyone, I smeared some icing on him, and he took some and put it on my cheek before licking it off.

I freaked out.

I assumed that was just good, hostile banter, but I later learned that he was on a mission. I told him he wasn't boyfriend material, which prompted him to pursue me. And the more arrogant and uninterested he appeared to be, the more I fell for him.

I was with a friend who lived with me at my mother's home. She left the party in the Hills before me. I went out to look for her and saw her kissing Danny. He pushed her away, and I could tell they were talking, but I felt enraged, thinking, Danny, you're such a pig. You were just macking on me, and when I walked out, you were kissing my friend.

A few weeks later, he told me that my buddy had completely taken him by surprise, most likely on purpose, because she knew I would be looking for her. Danny felt ashamed.

D'bat was dressed in the New Romantic style, with earrings, silk blouses, necklaces, bandannas, and feathers. My father was extremely charismatic; everyone spoke about him. He was really attractive, rode a bright red Kawasaki GPz550, and all of the girls adored him.

And, like my mother, he couldn't care less about fame; he might even be allergic to it, like she was.

My father initially saw my mother while repairing his motorcycle in the Celebrity Centre parking lot, and she was strolling across it with her mother. She was wearing a black leather jacket, and he wondered, "Who is that person with such an attitude?" As she passed, their gazes connected, and he had the impression she was looking directly at him.

My father was a jazz fan, and he had no idea Elvis had a daughter, let alone that the young woman in the black leather jacket was the child.

The next time he saw her was at the Mustache Café. Initially, my parents did not get along. "So, you think you're hot shit, huh?" my mother asked that night, alluding to his reputation. He simply felt she was aloof.

But he also thought that this little creature at the end of the table possessed such strength and presence, and it had nothing to do with being Elvis Presley's child. (In reality, they never talked about Elvis during their relationship—he knew she was devastated by his death, but she never mentioned it.) He realized right once that she didn't feel the need to impress anyone—and he also thought she was extremely physically attractive, with an intensity that drew him in.

The lighthearted rat-a-tat continued throughout dinner until he realized, "I kind of like this person." He claims he formed a crush on her due to her unattainable characteristics. My father replies, "She didn't just lie down and acquiesce to things. She was really feisty and could hold her own--not simply be disagreeable. I enjoyed the verbal sword fighting. "When she said I wasn't boyfriend material, it made me want her even more."

I was never one for short-term relationships or one-night hookups. If I'm into someone, I'm into them; if not, I'm not. Hot or chilly.

After another party a little later, I drove Danny home to his apartment, where he was renting a room in some strange neighborhood of Los Angeles, possibly Highland Park. His roommate, a twenty-three-year-old lady, was in the Witness Protection Program because she had exposed a major heroin dealer in Denver.

I recall going into his room and hanging around, talking, and spending the night there. Nothing occurred. We did not engage in any sexual activity. I just laid with him, making out and talking. I stayed till the early hours of the morning, then drove home alone.

My father recalls the night differently: "We had some drinks and were wrestling, throwing stuff around, and we knocked an old closet down and broke it." But my roommate couldn't be harsh because she was hiding.

After that, Danny and I formed a relationship. I was still being very careful. He had left a trail of broken hearts; he constantly broke up with the women, but they remained in love with him. His longest relationship had lasted six weeks. He was young, but I was even younger, so he was still more mature than I was. I was attempting to turn my life around--buckling down, getting my act together, getting over my manic phase and early drug use. I had not been a drug addict. I was just very curious and would do whatever came along.

It was really just rebellion.

You need something bigger than the surge drugs provide, bigger than that emotion, bigger than that bliss, bigger than that emptiness. And that is what I was beginning to develop. I wanted to know what the hell I was doing here, what life was like, and who these people were. I didn't want to fuck around anymore.

But I wasn't going to acquire a job, put food on the table, and be satisfied.

I needed answers.

Danny's self-assurance and arrogance appealed to me. I am drawn to powerful alpha dudes. That presumably comes from my father. My father was the alpha, and I am a complete daddy's girl. Even if I'm a very strong woman, that doesn't imply I want to wear trousers or call the shots. I don't mind if someone fills that role.

Danny and I dated for approximately four months at first, which was the longest he'd ever been with anyone, but I was concerned that Danny had a wandering eye. He might be a slippery son of a bitch, difficult to maintain hold of. I was madly in love with him, but he developed feelings for an Italian girl who didn't speak English and had hairy armpits. We were pretty much done after that.

But I always felt as if I was holding on to him. After we split up, I was distraught for two years and obsessed with him. Stuck and obsessed. I was one of the gals. I did not want anyone to know, but I was obsessed with him.

The Italian girl was only transient, but I was distraught. You couldn't clean me up from the floor.

Meanwhile, I'd date other uninteresting time-passers. Brock the Bug Squasher, for example, would get an erection from dropping potato bugs and watching them splatter. That was horrible, but Brock was also really attractive and in AA. I just used the Bug Squasher to annoy Danny. But everyone I dated knew I was still in love with Danny and that I was carrying the torch for him.

I wasn't sure what I wanted except to be with Danny. And I knew I needed to have children with Danny, which was the strangest and craziest part of it. I felt as if I was meant to have children with him--I knew we'd always be connected, that everything would be fine, and that it would never be a poor environment for a child.

Danny left Los Angeles for a while, and after he returned, my antennas were trained on him. I'd see him at parties, and it would break my heart, especially if he showed up with a lady. I didn't know what he was thinking about me. For a while, it was a game of cat and mouse: I'd go to a party with a guy, knowing Danny was there. I was completely devious, manipulative, and calculating. When Danny saw me with a guy, his entire demeanor changed; he'd be plainly disappointed, and his energy would drop. But I still didn't believe he genuinely cared.

She pursued him for two years. She was not ashamed. But he was only scared of her renown, and he was fleeing the phenomena because he knew she would destroy him.

He wasn't afraid of anything when he was younger, but she terrified the snot out of him.

He felt like a minnow in a shark-infested ocean. He was only a bass player. This was much too big.

I came up to his house one day and we sat on the curb outside to talk. I responded: "This is really eating me up, so let's just talk about how we actually feel, no more games." We were open with one other, and a few weeks later, we went on a date to the MTV Video Music Awards.

Danny nearly got arrested that night. At one point, a guy--a paparazzo, it turned out--came charging at us in the dark, and Danny impulsively attacked him, knocking him over one of those sawhorse barricades. We had to send a photo to People magazine so that the photographer would not file charges. They paid $70.000 for it.

We did not believe becoming famous was cool. We didn't really interact with other celebs. We were understated and unpretentious. I had to downplay things for Danny since he was so proud, and I didn't want to put him off. He would perform odd jobs such as painting, roofing, and construction, as well as playing whatever gigs came his way.

I did not live like a princess, either. My first car was a second hand Toyota Celica Supra.

However, one night at the China Club, I was sitting in a booth with my pals when Rick James jumped right next to me. Rick and I had seen one other a few times before, and he simply appeared so broken. He'd remark things like "Ugh, I'm not doing so well," such as "I'm trying to quit and I'm trying to get my life together." I had a warm spot for him. I wanted to fix him.

That night, Rick was high as fuck, and Danny shook his head when he got too close to me. Something went wrong, so Rick rose up and jumped through the air like a crazy beast to attack Danny. Fortunately, the bouncer noticed it and caught Rick in midair, throwing him out of the bar.

Around that time, I took a position as Jerry Schilling's assistant. Jerry was on the board of Elvis Presley Enterprises at the time, and my mother required me to attend meetings. I had no idea what the heck I was supposed to be doing, so I would just sit and listen. My mother was in charge, and she wanted me to be prepared to take over when I turned twenty-five.

I once made the mistake of sitting at the head of the table at a board meeting. My mother stepped in and said, "Don't ever sit in my seat at the head of the table." Who do you believe you are? This is my business; I am the one who founded Graceland. "You can't just walk in and sit there like you're something!"

But funny things happened during my short time working with Jerry Schilling as well. He was managing Jerry Lee Lewis at the time, who was the absolute worst person to manage. But Lewis loved me and was always kind to me.

One day, I was flying back from Memphis to Los Angeles and happened to sit next to Jerry Lee. When we landed, the office received a message from me aboard the plane saying, "Do not get off. Don't take his luggage. There are federal agents waiting for him at the gate.

Jerry Lee apparently had a briefcase, which I assume contained medications, most likely Demerol. Instead of grabbing the suitcase, Jerry Lee and I ran out of the airport like fugitives.

But I'm not a phone person--the worst thing you can do is force me to answer the phone. I used to answer the phone for Jerry Schilling.

He fired me after around six months.

Danny and I stayed together for a year. A full year. I was 19. I even claimed to enjoy his hero, bassist Jaco Pastorius, despite the fact that I was not a jazz enthusiast.

And I became pregnant in the year Danny and I were together. However, this was not the first time he had gotten me pregnant.

The first time I became pregnant, I had no idea. During the first four months we dated, I ended up in the ER with excruciating symptoms, and they rushed me into surgery. The doctors believed it was my appendix, but when I came around, they told me I had an ectopic pregnancy (they also removed my appendix).

I'd never gotten pregnant with another person, which is fascinating because I'd been just as irresponsible, not using birth control or anything. But with Danny, it happened the first time, and then again when we got back together.

That second time, neither I nor Danny knew what to do. I ended up getting an abortion. And it was the craziest thing I had ever done in my life. I was devastated. I did it, and we both cried. We were both destroyed, and shortly after, we came apart and split up. I could not live with myself.

Danny left to join the band on a cruise ship sailing through the Caribbean. I spent a couple of months traveling over Europe with a Eurail Pass. I couldn't believe I'd had an abortion. I was very unhappy with myself.

So I devised a plan.

I planned, plotted, and schemed. I knew exactly when I was ovulating; I even traveled to Memphis first to meet with my aunt Patsy and figure out how to make it happen. It was a joint effort. I got it down to a science and purposefully arranged a trip to see Danny aboard the ship.

We spent the night in Aruba or somewhere.

I remember getting back on the ship, praying I had fucking done it.

Danny had no idea about my strategy. But I no longer cared what he thought about it. I didn't care if he wanted to be a part of it or not. I felt compelled to redeem myself, to make amends, since I couldn't believe I'd had an abortion. I thought I was going to have this child. There is a child I need to have. I'd be talking to the missing child, saying, "I'm so sorry; I can't believe I fucking did that. Please forgive me and remain with me until I become pregnant again."

Then I left Aruba, waited two weeks, and took the pregnancy test. I called Danny up.

"I'm pregnant," I explained.

Danny knew he needed to marry me. I trapped him. I didn't intend to, but I did.

My mother then told me in detail how she timed her ovulation at that specific moment in Aruba. And she clearly intended to trap my father.

My father had been rehearsing in the disco room on the day he learned he was going to become a father. The ship was swaying back and forth, and he was gripping the drummer's cymbal to keep it from crashing down.

A greenroom was located to the right of the disco room, and someone called from there, "There's a phone call for you, Danny." This was long before cell phones, and phoning a ship was extremely uncommon; you had to call a relay point to connect to the boat using wideband radio. Or something like that.

When my father picked up the phone (he remembers it being white), my mother blurted, "I'm pregnant," and my father dropped the handset. He was shocked because he had never intended to marry or have children. But something made him say, "Let's do it."

So he soon recovered, took up the phone, and said quietly, "Okay."

My mother was not impressed; Danny was simply a really attractive wild musician with no real work or future. This was not what a parent would want for their child. She said I needed someone more famous and established.

One day at her house, her current lover (Edwards was no longer in the picture) took Danny to the tennis court, and when they returned, Danny was pale. Nobody knew what the hell that boyfriend did; he was constantly busy with meetings, but no one knew what they were about; he was incredibly Machiavellian. That day on the tennis court, the guy informed Danny that when I was finished with him, he would lose all of his aspirations and goals because this thing was so much bigger than him, that I didn't care or love him.

The boyfriend claimed that it wasn't love, but possession.

There were several attempts to separate my father from my mother in order to acquire control of her, the first of which occurred on the tennis court.

My mother was all emotion—she could feel her way through anything, but she wasn't cerebral. People were afraid of my father because he was extremely educated. He was an issue since he made it more difficult to control her. There were attempts to abort me, pursue him, and incriminate him, but he always came back swinging (until it nearly killed him to protect her).

While my father was on tour, the lover hired private investigators to research his past, and he told my mother that what they discovered was so dreadful and dark that he couldn't even tell her. When my father returned from the tour, my mother was quite distant and chilly toward him; when my father discovered why, he and my mother immediately went to meet with the boyfriend.

"You have my permission to tell Lisa everything you've found out about me," my father stated. But there had been nothing, of course, and the boyfriend mumbled something about "a mistake" before swiftly leaving the room.

I was terrified at this point; it felt like Danny and I were up against the entire world. But I remained pregnant, and we married at the

Celebrity Centre, with only my mother, a preacher, and a few close friends in attendance.

About six months later, we had a large wedding reception at the Bel-Air Country Club. I donned a white dress for my family and friends to make everyone feel included.

I was already pretty pregnant at the time.

I was dealing with baby weight and getting slammed in the news for it. They used to label you overweight when you were pregnant. I couldn't bear having so many paparazzi following me and focusing on my pregnancy. I was continuously harassed. For the first time, I was involved in a car chase, driving erratically to get rid of them. Just going to the supermarket.

Danny and I purchased our first home, a normal house in the Valley. We were prepared to have our baby, but the pressure was definitely the worst I'd ever experienced.

The police assisted us in and out of the hospital. It was also stressful to try to deliver a child while having to post security and police officers on the floor, with the paparazzi trying to come in and the police trying to get us out, similar to how they try to get the president out of a building.

My parents perpetrated a joke on the paparazzi who had gathered at our modest Tarzana home, right on the street, on the day of my birth. We had no gate security or anything back then. My father had a buddy who lived on Sunny Cove, a small cul-de-sac off Mulholland Drive in Hollywood Hills. My father knew the paparazzi would follow them to the hospital, so he called his friend when my mother went into labor, and they drove up to the end of Sunny Cove with the media in tow. My parents managed their escape after a buddy drove out and blocked the street.

My mom and dad had attended Lamaze classes. They gave them a focal pyramid—that's their go-to move—and you're supposed to place it where the woman can focus on it.

My mother was screaming in pain when she went into labor with me, but she chose not to get an epidural right away. My father was attempting to help, encouraging her to concentrate on the pyramid.

"Fuck the pyramid, and fuck you!" she exclaimed.

My parents named me Riley, but they couldn't think of a middle name. Priscilla's mother, Ann (called Nana), proposed I be named after my father. My parents had no other options, so they left it to the hospital, where someone decided Danielle sounded better than Riley, which is why my government name is Danielle Riley Keough.

Photographers entered the room shortly after my birth and took pictures. There was pressure on my mother to release a photo of me so that the journalists would stop following us. The photograph was valued at $300,000, which was an even larger sum of money in the 1980s, and is equivalent to about a million dollars today. It appeared on the cover of People magazine, with the caption "ELVIS'S FIRST GRANDCHILD." Here she is!

And then I had a crash course in motherhood.

Like my mother, I married at twenty and became a mother at twenty-one.

But when Riley was born, everyone was overjoyed. She was a one-of-a-kind spirit, a beacon of light in the universe. I believe I was a vessel fulfilling another purpose: Riley was mine, but she was also for everyone else.

I fell in love with being a mother. I knew I was called to care for something else. Being a mother meant everything to me, and Riley was the most precious treasure. I was going to do all possible to protect and raise her.

That thing where you either do what your parents did or do the complete opposite of what they did to you? I did the opposite.

Danny joined a band named Ten Inch Men and began performing around town. I developed a crush on the lead singer (the guy had significant lead singer syndrome), which caused problems in our marriage. Drunk one night, the singer told me, "You know, if it weren't for Danny, I think you and I'd be perfect together." I told Danny what he had said; I was always truthful with him. But it was difficult because Danny would be onstage, while I would be watching the main singer. It drove Danny insane and led to the band's disbandment.

Danny began taking mushrooms and smoking pot, which was causing major disputes between us because I had become very anti-drug by that point.

But, for the most part, we had things under control.

We moved into a home on Mountaingate, above the 405. We were simply a regular married couple. We were holding family parties and barbecues.

Now we three are living above the 405 in Los Angeles. It's 1991.

"Jaco ran away!"

That's my earliest memory.

My father runs, and my mother runs. I am in her arms. She repeatedly shouts, "Jaco ran away! Jaco ran away!" that's as if mentioning that implies it might not be true. She's quite upset. We are running along our street. Normally, I might hear cars on the 405 freeway down in the canyon, but today all I hear is my mother crying, "Jaco ran away! Jaco ran away!"

Jaco was our Pug. They named him after Jaco Pastorius. My father once met the great Jaco at Stanley Clarke's house on his birthday. Jaco arrived in a late-model Mercedes; he wasn't yet homeless or utterly addicted to narcotics. He had already produced the iconic albums with Joni Mitchell and Weather Report. My father was sixteen when he met his idol.

Now he's ten years older and pursuing a new Jaco down the street.

We never found Jaco. Perhaps he was taken by a neighbor or a coyote? My parents were not particularly responsible back then, but they adored me. I never doubted it. Ever.

That was what my mother had felt about Elvis. That is how she wanted me to feel.

However, the lead singer's infatuation was really difficult for my father because his two zones—family and band—had been disrupted.

After one trip, my father returned and revealed that he had briefly hooked up with a set of twins while he was abroad. He didn't have sex with them—he was proud that it was only kissing and sexy dancing—but he informed my mother. She tossed a dish across the kitchen like a Frisbee at his head.

Many years later, they discussed it in front of me, and here's what happened:

Mom: Are there two of them? I assumed it was one.

Dad: Maybe this is a different situation.

Mom: I didn't know about the twins.

Dad: They weren't twins. They were two friends. Mom: Ah, two pals...

My parents received death threats shortly after we moved into that residence. There was one guy in particular, a hill guy from the South- -my father said he had no teeth and was seven feet tall--who was sending letters stating he was coming to fetch me since, supposedly, I was his daughter. "I'm going to kill Danny and get my child back," he wrote from deep within Arkansas. My father moved me and my mother to Hawaii and sat in our house with a rifle in his lap, waiting for him. My parents had private investigators track the man down when he arrived in town, but the authorities could only keep him for a few days in Los Angeles. As a result, the gun was created.

Another time, my father called the police to report that there was a man with a pistol outside our house. They arrived and stomped him to the ground, and he later sued my father.

Following that, we lived primarily in gated neighborhoods. We had to.

I enjoyed being a mother so much that I wanted another child, and I really wanted a boy. My mother had advised me on how to have a boy or a girl. Essentially, she stated that boy sperm arrives sooner than girl sperm but dies faster, therefore if you want a boy, you must have intercourse shortly before the commencement of your ovulation (to get the first sperm alone).

So, just like when I scheduled that vacation to get pregnant the first time, I was determined to have a boy this time, and I had to plan it, which meant we only had a limited timeframe. We did it three times in one day before stopping since I didn't want to risk female sperm going in there.

When I became pregnant, we traveled to Florida and rented a property there. The pregnancy was pretty uncomplicated. I was in excellent form at the time because I worked out frequently. I aimed for an increase of exactly twenty-six pounds, which is what I required to have a healthy baby, and sure enough, I gained exactly twenty-six pounds, all in my belly.

When my water broke, we traveled to Tampa, where I had my baby, Ben, naturally. We lived in Florida for almost a year and a half, and everything was fine--we were both really calm at that point. It felt settled.

But then I started taking voice lessons.

The more severe the weather, the happier my mother grew.

When you live in Florida, it seems like there's a tornado or hurricane warning every week - Mother Nature is powerful there. My mother enjoyed the harsh weather. Even though she had lived in Southern California on and off for most of her life, she despised the weather there. She disliked sunshine until she was on a beach in Hawaii. My mother desired snow, rain, and tropical storms...just something.

I was sitting in the Tampa hospital waiting room with my father's brother, Thomas, and his wife, Eve, on the day of my brother's birth. It was late and dark. The next thing I remember is being in my mother's hospital room, where I feel dwarfed by the bed's height. I am staring up. It is quiet. My mother and father are present, as is my new brother. I don't recall touching Ben, but I do remember the essence of simply being there, that nighttime newborn feeling that filled the room.

I'd always wanted to sing, but I never did. I only attended the classes to warm up my voice, but one day I urged my teacher to turn around and not look at me.

I replied, "Just listen, and if you believe I have a chance at this, or if you think there's anything in me that should pursue it, please let me know. If not, we'll pretend this never occurred."

With that, I sang a line and chorus of Aretha Franklin's "Baby I Love You."

When the woman turned around, she appeared genuinely stunned. She had her husband and some other people come in, and then she made me do it again. Despite knowing what I was up against, I thought, "Wow." Maybe I can do it...

I asked Danny to produce this tune for me. I commented on him: "I'll either do this and it's going to work out, or it's going to be the biggest embarrassment of my life and we'll just pretend like it didn't happen."

Danny produced "Baby I Love You" at the famed One on One studio in Los Angeles. (Danny had previously worked there, but was dismissed for failing to answer the phone because he was too busy playing bass.) I passed the recording around to my family. Everyone's mouth dropped—they couldn't believe it was my voice. So Danny and I began writing music together, and I recorded a demo cassette. And then word spread, and Prince, Michael Jackson, and everyone else began swarming in.

That demo tape altered our lives forever.

Chapter 5: Mimi

I met Michael Jackson when I was a little girl in Las Vegas. I believe I was about six. My father was performing at the Hilton, and the Jackson Five were playing down the street. Michael remembers that I went backstage to meet them. I don't recall it at all.

When I was a teenager, maybe fifteen or sixteen, Michael invited my mother to meet him for supper. When I noticed the texts he had left, I asked, "Mom, what the fuck are you doing? "Why is Michael Jackson calling you?" Later, I learned that he had hoped I would accompany her. He didn't state it explicitly since he didn't want it to seem strange.

Then, a few years later, while I was working for Jerry Schilling and managing Jerry Lee Lewis, Michael attempted to reach me through a businessman named John Branca, who worked for the Elvis estate but also assisted Michael in acquiring the Beatles' library. But at the time, I was going to marry Danny, so nothing happened. Michael subsequently informed me that when I appeared on the cover of People magazine after Danny and I married, he was upset. He felt that he should be with me instead.

I had no idea what was going on.

I first met Michael in 1993, following his Super Bowl halftime performance and interview with Oprah. We connected through a common buddy. I had a demo tape out, and he said he had heard it and wanted to see me. I did not want to go at first. I did not want to be someone else's project. Prince had also done it, and while I appreciated what they were doing, I wanted to do my own thing.

I went anyway.

When Michael arrived, I was surprised to see him alone, and even more so because he was so calm and pleasant. Danny was with me and had everyone leave the room so Michael and I could talk.

We just clicked. We swapped phone numbers, and he called me. I was living in Clearwater at the time, working hard on Scientology and making progress. Back then, I wouldn't even take Advil, which is ridiculous. But Michael would call. We had devised a signal: if the phone rang three times and then stopped, it was Michael, and you had to clear the fuck out of the way so I could speak with him. We'd be on the phone for extended amounts of time. I just assumed he was lonely and needed a friend. But he was after me.

He eventually invited me to visit him in Atlanta, and I traveled with my assistant, who happened to be Danny's brother's wife. There, I exclusively hung out with Michael. We visited amusement parks. I don't know why Danny let me do it or why he trusted me.

Mistake.

This carried on for a few months until the molestation charges surfaced. Michael left and went into hiding. Nobody could find him. I made it clear that I was available if he wanted to talk to me. He called me almost every other day. I was one of only a few people that spoke to him or knew where he was.

He sought treatment in Switzerland for prescription drugs before returning to Los Angeles. That's when the Northridge earthquake struck, and I heard Michael hurried out of his house in his pajamas, jumped into his Jeep, went to the airport, and flew to Las Vegas on a Gulfstream because he was scared of earthquakes.

I thought that was hilarious.

He called from Vegas and asked me to join him again. I went to the Mirage, where he was staying, and I brought the kids and my sister-in-law along. Michael and I had different rooms, but every night I'd go to his room, and we'd spend the night talking as you do when you first meet someone, watching movies like Jaws, drinking, and talking about our childhoods, lives, and how we felt.

Michael had vitality and presence, and that week he fully let me inside his universe, his intellect. I knew he didn't do that very often. I don't believe he ever did, until we started talking. He knew I understood him, and we had a strong connection since I did not condemn him. I absolutely understand who he was and why he thought what he did. We had come from and were presently in similar situations. Everything about our lives was absolutely abnormal. There was no reason why we should not communicate.

And what about that meeting as children? He remembered every detail, including where I sat and what I said.

"You remember the white dress?" he asked.

I asked, "How do you remember the white dress I wore? My god. Do you remember? I don't recall any of this. All I remember was being terrified to tell my father that I wanted to see someone else's show.

I was only scheduled to be in Vegas for two days, but I ended up staying for eight. Nothing happened physically, but the connection was quite intense. Nobody had ever seen that side of him. He wasn't the high-pitched, calculated type. That was an act.

Danny flew to Las Vegas and tried to find us in the Mirage by banging on doors. I told Danny that I was merely helping Michael as a friend, and that he should leave us alone and go home. And that is exactly what he did.

Michael invited me back to his room on the final night. When I came, he remarked, "Don't stare at me; I am quite frightened. "I want to tell you something," he said before turning off the lights.

And in the darkness, Michael remarked, "I'm not sure if you've noticed, but I'm completely in love with you." "I want us to marry and you to have my children." He then played me a song about how he felt, and when he was done, he said, "You don't have to say anything. I realize I've thrown you off, but I genuinely want you. "I want to be with you."

I didn't say anything right away, but I soon said, "I'm really so flattered, I can't even talk." By then, I had fallen in love with him as well. I'd informed him that my marriage was in serious peril.

I was holding it all in, so when I returned to my hotel at the Mirage, I just lost it. I recall walking into the closet, leaning against the wall, and simply staring. I was intrigued and shaken.... Oh my fucking God, what had just happened?

I didn't want to tell him I felt the same way since I was with my two children, and I needed to go home and tell my husband first. But I was also madly in love.

The next morning, Michael and I flew back to Los Angeles aboard a private jet. When we landed, Michael said, "I'll miss you." And then he said he'd leave it up to me to decide what to do, and he'd call me.

When I arrived home, Danny was asleep in his bed. I was all made up. Every time I saw Michael, I had my hair done, wore an outfit, and had my nails done; everything was flawless.

Her nails were fire-engine red, and she tapped them angrily on the glass coffee table. I'd try to copy her, but I was too small to have noisy nails.

My mother was a nail biter; she'd bite them almost to the cuticle, resulting in bloody nails that she didn't want Michael to see. She wanted to be the ideal lady for him—Michael had no idea my mother smoked, for example—which was not unlike how her mother had been with her father. But after she and Michael had been together for a long time, he finally told her that he liked her nails best when they were natural--he didn't expect her to be the perfect lady. She couldn't believe she'd spent thousands of dollars on nails in a year, and he preferred bitten ones.

So there I was, all dressed up, despite having not slept all night.

Danny responded, "Come and get in bed with me."

"Actually, I can't do that," I answered before leaving the room.

Danny came to find me.

"Let's talk," he suggested. "What happened?"

"Well," my response was, "Michael asked me to leave you and marry him and have children with him."

"What did you say?"

"I said nothing."

"That's it, then," Danny replied. "That is it. "Forget it."

Then Danny packed his things, grabbed the dog, and drove out the darn gate.

Gone.

Within a day, Michael called. Was I leaving Danny, or not? When Michael learned what had transpired, he became ecstatic and sent massive flower arrangements. I started visiting him in Los Angeles. I was usually nervous. I recall sweating profusely.

He told me that he was still a virgin. I believe he kissed Tatum O'Neal, and he had a thing with Brooke Shields that wasn't physical other than the kiss. He claimed Madonna had attempted to hook up with him once before, but nothing transpired.

I was afraid because I did not want to make the incorrect decision. When he decided to kiss me first, he did so. He was instigating everything. I was astonished when the physical things began to happen. I had assumed that we wouldn't do anything until we married, but he responded, "I'm not waiting!"

I was sitting on my mother's lap in a hotel room in Clearwater, Florida, when she informed me that she and my father were getting divorced. I was upset, sobbing uncontrollably because I feared that meant he was no longer my father.

"No, no, of course he is your dad," my mother said.

That day, Ben found one of her bright red lipsticks and drew a huge line across the wall. He had always enjoyed playing with her cosmetics, but this time he was going to get in a lot of trouble.

"I'm going to tell you," I announced, and I did.

I remember hearing Ben being yelled at in the other room and weeping, and I felt terrible. For years, I felt the shame of being the older sibling.

Ben could always shatter my heart.

Michael seems to have hit home with my mother. She wanted to fix him because she believed he was misunderstood, which she was quite familiar with.

My dad was devastated. Following his divorce from my mother, dad spent three months traveling across Italy on a yacht with his pals before heading down to Mexico. He read Bukowski's recently released poem "The Bluebird," which reminded him of my mother. He became trapped in a jungle while hallucinating from a drink supplied to him by locals and was eventually rescued by a dog named Searchlight. When he returned, he had a tattoo, black eyes, and orange hair. I cried when I saw him because I could feel his pain. My brother rushed into his bedroom and grabbed an eraser to try to remove the tattoo.

When we entered the lawyer's office together, Danny stated, "I don't want anything." There was no prenup, but I told him he had to take something, so I pushed him to accept a small sum of money.

Danny was outstanding in that regard. He never betrayed me. He's always been there for me. He basically filed the divorce paperwork so that I could marry Michael.

We were best pals. We spent every family trip together. Riley and Ben never noticed anything wrong between us. We made it fantastic for them.

My brother couldn't pronounce Michael's name, so we called him "Mimi". Michael was larger than life and reminded her of her father. She told me that no one, except Michael, came close to being like her father.

We weren't sure if they were in a love connection or if she was just bringing a buddy around. (I like to joke that she was always quite good at introducing her children to their numerous husbands.) We would hang out and do activities with Mimi, as we had with others, long before she told us they were in a relationship.

I don't remember when she informed me they were getting married, but I do recall he started sleeping over.

When he came over, her entire world came to a halt. The front gate would chime, and a voice would announce, "MJ is here." The journey from the gate to our house took about six minutes, and my mother would be rushing about to fix her lips and put on lipstick.

He would enter our kitchen through the back door. Typically, the kitchen counter was covered in heaps of NDAS and tabloids laid out for her by her assistants--OK!, Star, National Enquirer, Globe--so my mother could read all the cover stories about herself. When Michael came to visit, she didn't leave the magazines out or require him to sign an NDA. He was probably the sole exception.

Michael and my mother immediately became well-known. When big events in our lives occurred that would cause the press to go crazy, she would pull us out of school and force us to stay at home until the situation calmed down. When we returned to school, we had security outside all day. And if I went to a sleepover at a friend's house, security would sit outside all night as well. My mother was deeply touched by what others said about her. She didn't have any siblings to share the load with, and no one knew how she felt. In some ways, she was America's princess, even if she did not want to be.

Her resistance simply made the chase more attractive to the media. There were photographers among the woods. My father was constantly pushing or battling some paparazzi.

She had fought her entire life to get away from it. Despite this, she fell for Michael Jackson.

When Michael entered our lives, his reputation grew rapidly. I don't believe anyone anticipated the scale of it. My mother definitely didn't. She rarely considered the repercussions.

Michael and my mother married in the Dominican Republic, twenty days after she divorced my father. She subsequently told Playboy magazine that she hadn't told her mother about it until Priscilla called and said, "There are helicopters hovering over my house, driving me nuts. "They say you married Michael Jackson."

My mother just stated, "Yup, I did."

I was honestly very happy.

I've never felt so thrilled again.

We married in the Dominican Republic on the DL. There were two witnesses.

Then it was just the two of us, alone. We'd be running from one rented property to the next. We'd get into a lot of trouble. He'd occasionally summon his main security guard to join us, but we'd wind up dumping him because we wanted to be alone, even if it meant wandering into risky regions. But we just wanted to be alone, normal, and anonymous. I would do his laundry, and we would run errands and go shopping together. We rented a quaint small cottage in Orlando's gay area for our honeymoon, and we'd go around and look at real estate while visiting Disney World every other day.

He wasn't doing any drugs at the time. We stayed up all night, talking sober.

Michael was an incredible conversationalist. He despised talking about himself, so he would usually be distracted. He was very interested in people and could really lift them up. He'd do whatever to redirect the topic back to you and what you were doing; he'd be captivated by all you had to say about your work. There was an energy there, something about him that was absolutely exceptional, that I had never seen or felt before in my life, save with my father.

I felt quite fortunate that he let me in.

I fell in love with him because he was completely regular. Nobody saw his usual side. His mother would exclaim, "He told you that stuff?" and Janet would respond, "I've never heard him talk about anything like that." I wished he'd exhibit that side more. He didn't talk much to his brothers at the time, and I believe they were startled that our relationship was legitimate. But they thought it was awesome.

Nobody had ever seen him with his guard down. I knew it was rare. With everyone else, he would snap his fingers if someone spoke something he didn't like - snap, and you're out. Because he could make his own world. In that universe, everyone had to agree with what he said.

But in our world, I would express my feelings, and he liked that in me because it wasn't directed at him. I could be honest without hiding anything. He knew I was a lioness around my children and everyone I loved. He'd make me deal with them and be the evil cop. He accepted my feelings and typically agreed with me about the people around him and the trash that was going on.

He adored that aspect of me until we got into a fight and I told him the truth, which was toward the end.

Michael resided with us in Hidden Hills. We occasionally stayed in Neverland, but he was mostly at our place. In Hidden Hills, the call of wild coyotes would put me to sleep, but in Neverland, I'd wake up to a pet giraffe outside my window.

At home, they were a typical married couple. They would drive us to school together every morning, just like any other family, but Michael would occasionally bring a chimpanzee.

Before you ask, it wasn't Bubbles.

He would frequently sing to us. He used to sing "Happy Birthday, Lisa" by Bart Simpson to my mother. To Ben, he'd sing "Ben," his first solo number one single. And to me, he'd sing "You Are Not Alone."

One day, Ben was riding the oak tree swing in his diaper--he frequently wore only his diaper or no clothes at all--and he was flying high. He said, "Look, Mimi! "Look, Mimi!" he exclaimed, anxious to show Michael how high he was swinging and amaze him. But Michael was too busy playing with me. My brother fell backward, struck his head on the ground, and started crying. We all rushed over to check on him.

The next day, he decided to poop under the swing in protest.

After marrying Michael, my mother traveled with ten security guards. When we were driving around, people would hurl their bodies at us, smashing into the windows, yelling, and attempting to grab us. My brother turned to me once and exclaimed excitedly, "They're following us!" I said to him, "They're following Mimi."

We were not permitted to go outside without a hat or sunglasses on. I'm not sure what they expected, but I remember my mother and Michael laughing so hard one day when I came into her wardrobe to find her trying on a really long red wig. They were both wearing wigs in the naive hope that she and Michael would be able to blend in with the rest of the world.

My mother and Michael were constantly sassy to each other. They spoke to each other in the same way Delta and Patsy did. Both brought with them generational drug difficulties, and both came from impoverished backgrounds: Vernon was a sharecropper and carpenter, and Joe Jackson worked as a crane operator. And Michael and my mother's father knew all too well what it was like to have godlike fame, which seemed to emerge overnight.

My mother felt right at home among Michael's family members. She enjoyed eating dinner at Hayvenhurst with them.

Michael had wanted children with my mother since they first met, but she was never certain. She did not have the same feeling she had with my father. From the beginning, their marriage was marked by a fundamental disagreement about whether or not to have children. Michael would occasionally declare, "If you're not going to have children with me, then I'm going to find somebody who will." He would also remark, "Debbie Rowe has told me she will have my children."

My mother would retort jealously, "Then go fuck Debbie Rowe." I just knew Debbie as a compassionate lady who assisted me with my ear problems.

When Michael called me following the charges, he informed me that Evan Chandler, the father of one of the accusers, was extorting him, and I believe I persuaded him to settle it; everyone recommended him to pay because it would be a fucking nightmare.

Regarding child molestation, I've never seen anything like it. Personally, I would have killed him.

I didn't want to be on the front lines or make any headlines. I grew up avoiding and hating the press. I conducted an interview with Diane Sawyer in 1995 to protect him. I thought he needed me, which I liked. It was wonderful for me to be able to play the female role for once, allowing me to care for my husband.

Chandler sued me after that interview because Michael had signed a confidentiality agreement with him and had been advised not to bring up the matter, but I had never signed anything. So I would go right in and claim that the claims were false, and that is how I won the lawsuit. It came down to the deposition stage, but I won.

Michael's album HIStory was published in 1995. I was in the studio with him the entire time he was making it. When it came time for the pre-press, it was evident that he was under pressure. I started to see peculiarities in him.

For nearly a year, they were on a high from being freshly in love, and then everything went bad.

My mother began to suspect that Michael was using drugs, and she began to notice characteristics similar to those of her father.

He became increasingly secretive around her. She told me she believed he was shielding his addiction. My mother was quite anti-drug at the time, and she would later march on the streets of Washington, D.C., to protest the use of psychiatric medication in children. When she began asking more questions regarding his addiction, it caused a lot of conflict. They began fighting frequently, and he iced her for days. I know there was a really bad fight— someone threw a platter of fruit at somebody. They were two large spirits with tremendous tempers.

Paranoia developed in both of them, and they were surrounded by individuals whispering into their ears.

She had no idea he was going to kiss her at the 1994 MTV Video Music Awards until just before it happened. Eventually, the thought crossed her mind: Did he merely do that for the press? Was he just another version of her first boyfriend, who sold park photos? It created the suspicion that he was only there because she was Elvis' daughter, a novelty. She no longer trusted him. She believed Michael no longer trusted her, and he suspected she was catching on to his addiction.

Her distrust of everyone around her only deepened. Michael went missing for several days, and my mother had no idea where he was. She tried to reach out to his group, but no one would respond.

Michael began making frequent visits to the doctor's office. I'd take him up and he'd be completely out of it. I believe it was Demerol injections. He stated he required it for a scalp injury, but I felt there was more to the story, and it was significant. One of his family members informed me that it was a pill habit.

He was about to do a huge HBO thing, and I believe he didn't want to do it, so he pretended to fall and went to the hospital. I kept asking what was wrong with him, and each day I received a different response. Karen, his makeup artist, informed me that he had fully planned it since he didn't want to do the HBO thing.

I flew to New York, where he was hospitalized, and spent every day with him. His mother was also present, along with his team, which included his own anesthesiologist.

Nobody has their own anesthesiologist; each hospital has its own. This was a huge red flag. At first, I couldn't figure out what was going on, but I eventually realized: He wanted someone around who could legally give the medications. I informed one of the security personnel that I wanted to enter his bathroom to see what he was taking. A family member begged me to collect his urine and test it, but I declined.

Michael was being really rude; he became enraged at me for asking questions. I asked, "What is actually going on here? "If you have a problem, I will accompany you to rehab." The doctor began harassing me, threatening me, and urging me to stop asking so many questions. I replied: "I'm just trying to find out what's going on with my husband."

The doctor and Michael had a conversation, and when the doctor emerged from his room, he said, "He wants to talk to you."

In the room, Michael stated, "You're making too many difficulties. They'll transport you to the airport; you should stay at home until I'm done. I will see you when I get back."

So I left. I wanted him to join us, but he didn't.

I filed for divorce pretty soon after.

Someone had told my mother that Michael was going to file for divorce, but it would be better for her if she did it first. My mother told Oprah in 2010 that she decided to walk because she saw the medications and physicians come in, which worried her and reminded her of what she had gone through with her father.

So she filed. But the truth was that Michael never intended to file. Romeo and Juliet drank the poison by mistake. Michael was deeply hurt, and my mother tried and tried to contact him, calling and writing. But he refused to talk with her.

My mother always stated that Michael taught her how to freeze people. They eventually reconnected and began to hang out. They were involved in a back-and-forth, destructive relationship. He told her that he was going to marry Debbie because he wanted children. Their divorce was finalized in August 1996, and Michael and Debbie married three months later. But we would still visit Neverland.

I'm not sure what the atmosphere was between my mother and Michael--whether they were still hooking up or not--but we were definitely over there a lot.

We communicated for years.

He desperately wanted me to have his children, and I refused. I knew he wanted to be the sole caretaker of the children. Michael desired control over the situation. He didn't want to be influenced by his mother or anyone else.

I assumed Michael would have me have the children and then dump me, leaving me out of the picture. I could read him like a clock. I understood everything and knew everything about him because all we did was open our hearts to one another. I understood his personality; he was very controlling and calculating.

He once called me when he was at work. During the conversation, I said, "You're like a snake-I don't know what you're going to crawl out from under...."

Michael remarked, "Oh, that's fantastic. I call home and speak with my wife, who tells me I'm a snake.

"Well," I replied, "yes, you are."

In 1997, my mother brought us all to South Africa to see Michael perform for the last time. (We'd sit on the side of the stage as he sang, and he'd bring me and some other kids out onstage for "Heal the World.")

On the way to the show, our private plane nearly crashed, forcing us to make an emergency landing in a remote settlement. My mom saw the near-disaster as a bad omen.

After South Africa, my mother recognized she needed to end whatever this relationship had become. It was not good for her, so she cut Michael out of her life.

Years later, Michael called my mother. She stated he did not sound sober. He replied, "You were right. "Everyone around me wants to kill me."

This was their last discussion.

My mother was in London, writing a record, when Michael died. My mother later told Oprah that Michael regularly expressed fear of becoming like her father. He was always questioning my mother about Elvis' death, including when, how, where, and why. Michael stated, "I feel like I'm going to end up the same way."

My mother sat with Michael's casket for hours after everyone else had left, exactly as she had done with her father. She told Oprah that she didn't think she could make peace; instead, she wanted to apologize for not being present.

My mother informed me that she interacted with Michael in her nightmares for several months after he died.

Chapter 6: Ten Years

As I indicated in the preface, when my mother sat for the interviews that served as the foundation for this book, she was not in a position to recount all of the wonderful, enjoyable events in her life. She concentrated primarily on the trauma.

As a result, there is significantly less information on the tapes about the years between her divorce from Michael Jackson and her marriage to Michael Lockwood, a ten-year period during which she created a fantastic life for me and my brother while surrounded by a big group of dedicated friends. These years were some of the happiest of her life. However, they were also years when her life grew to almost unmanageable proportions.

Fortunately, my mother told me everything about her life (which, as a daughter, can often feel like a curse, but I was grateful she did when I was working on the book). So much of the information in this chapter is based on my recall of what she told me.

In Florida, we lived in a neighborhood called Belleair. There was a swampy, Southern vibe to the place, with fireflies, alligators, and moss-covered trees.

We lived in a large, old house. A bedroom is to the right of the entrance door, and I'm peeping through. The room is dark, with all of the shades drawn even though it is noon. I'm seeing my mom shushing my brother, who is on her shoulder. I remember the rhythm, sh-sh-sh, three notes repeated over and over.

I now realize that this was my first glimpse into the depth of her maternal instincts--my mother had the deepest such instincts of anyone I'd ever encountered. It would eventually become evident to me that if somebody hurt Ben or me, Mom would most likely chase them down for as long as it took, much like in a Western. This was the presence you could feel in her, and it was not insignificant. That was terrifying.

Something else terrifying: I only have happy memories of Ben, but my mother once told me that shortly after his birth, I said, "I wish all the babies in the world would die." Clearly, this was my way of expressing how sad I was about this baby.

I had a feeling Ben was the love of my mother's life.

My brother and I would often discuss how magical our childhoods were. Perhaps it was just the timing and location; perhaps we were simply fortunate to be present at such a great moment. What was certain was that we had exceptional parents who wanted us to have a happy upbringing.

My mother hired a nanny for each of us; I had Idy, a teenager, and Ben had Uant, a South African woman in her fifties. Uant was fantastic for him—they'd spend all day in the garden, watering plants and getting messy. Ben got a South African accent after learning to speak due to his constant interaction with Uant.

Ben had curly ringlets that reached his buttocks, and many people mistook him for a lady. He loved being outside, a little nature kid, and he was kind, delicate, and gentle, like an old soul.

My brother and my mother had a "I can't live without you" bond, much like Elvis did with his mother and my mother did with Elvis. They have a really profound soul bond.

Ben was quite similar to his grandfather in every regard, including his appearance. Ben looked so much like him that it worried me. I didn't want to inform him since I believed it was excessive for a child.

We were quite close—he would tell me everything. Ben and I shared the same bond that my father and his mother did. It was a fucking cycle that persisted throughout generations.

Gladys loved my father so much that she drank herself to death worried about him. And then my father had his demons and acted out on them. Every part of me wants to do the same thing. And then my son has the same genetic makeup--I believe he is more genetically me than Danny.

Ben did not stand a chance.

When I was approximately seven years old, we moved to a new house a little further north in Clearwater, on Osceola Avenue, with an oceanfront dock. Ben and I would leap off that dock into the mud when the tide was out, rolling our entire bodies in it, coating ourselves in this awful ocean ooze, and playing with the seaweed, dead fish, and shells. Some days, we'd go to locate lizards, and we discovered that if you pushed on one's belly, it would open its mouth, and when you let go, it would snap shut--which is how Ben could wear them as earrings. We had a pool in our backyard, and every day, my mother would cry from the house to get out when thunder and lightning struck, but we'd always try to stay in the water--it was more exciting when it rained and the sky lighted up.

My mother's favorite thing to do was take us to the park near the lake to play on the swings. (She preferred going on the swings rather than pushing us.) Her two regulations in Florida, which we heard frequently, were that you couldn't swim in the rain and that if an alligator followed you, you had to run in zig zags.

My mother would take us out onto Clearwater Harbor on Jet Skis, doing donuts and dumping everyone off the back. It was the same enthusiasm she'd felt at Graceland, with the golf carts going wild. She once threw her mother off the back, then terrified my grandma by imagining sharks were approaching her.

Other times, we'd cross the water to a small island covered in sand dollars. We'd gather them, bring them home, dry them, and then open Aristotle's lamp to reveal these small dove-like shapes that were actually their teeth, poor things.

I still feel horrible about the lizards and sand dollars. And my grandmother.

My mom would take me to the Sandcastle for frozen yogurt in a cone, just the two of us. She'd have the music blasting in her black Mercedes--always a black Mercedes--and we'd listen to Toad the Wet Sprocket (it was the 1990s) and Toni Braxton and Mark Morrison's "Return of the Mack," but my mother liked all R&B. My mother would always sing along in the car, but in a self-conscious manner, as if she did not want others to hear her. I didn't understand then why she was afraid of music.

My mother developed panic episodes following her divorce from Michael. This is why she took us from Los Angeles to Florida in the first place. They were so bad that she had to be hospitalized several times. Even in Florida, she had to cover the windows with aluminum foil to prevent photographers from taking shots of her. She had her gallbladder removed and the mercury removed from her teeth. However, nothing helped because the problem was more than just physical. She was having some type of mental breakdown.

Just as my mother used to pick up the phone to listen in on conversations between Elvis and Ginger Alden, I once unintentionally picked up the phone in Florida in time to hear my father--who had just seen a photo in the press of Michael Jackson, my mother, me, and Ben--say, "Get my son off that guy's fucking lap." I quickly hung up the telephone. Strangely, this was the first time I recognized my father was unhappy with my mother's marriage to Michael—that's how well they shielded us from their adult issues.

Despite his pain, my father saw that my mother needed assistance and flew to Florida to care for all of us.

She later informed me that was the last time they hooked up.

My mother urgently wanted to reconcile with my father. She believed she had broken up her family and felt terrible shame, but my father couldn't risk being so vulnerable again.

My father and his friends would sit on our house's balcony at night, playing and singing as tropical storms passed. My mother and father, along with the rest of us, sang "Leaving on a Jet Plane" when the rain was pouring down one night. Both of my parents adored rain and despised the sun; they chose my brother's middle name, Storm, during Tropical Storm Earl.

Growing up, I had no prototype to follow. I never had a family or a home life to set an example by. No stability. I had no emotional tie to my grandparents, who appeared to be wonderful, doing all the right things and making all the right moves, getting married, having children, and remaining married until death.

I assume I didn't have a chance in hell.

If something no longer interests me, I'll leave. And everytime you meet a new person, the entire experience—the beginning, middle, and end—will play out in two years. That is why I have married several times.

When I had Riley, I focused fully on having and raising a child. Was my aim for her to have stable parents, and were Danny and I going to be married forever? No fucking way. That was not something one of us considered. But we were not your typical soulmates, and we always ended up living in the same house.

My parents started recording music in my mom's garage in Florida. These would become some of the tracks on her debut LP. They'd write throughout the day, then at night we'd go have frozen yogurt or go to the movies (my mom always grabbed a medium popcorn and a red Icee).

She was usually quite protective of us, making sure we didn't watch anything too mature--I remember seeing Flubber at the local cinema, but I also recall being dragged to see Titanic. She kept her hands over my eyes during the sex session in the automobile. So I could see the sinking ship, but not the boobs. She acquired modesty from my grandmother.

Some days, she would take us to Clearwater's Dairy Kurl for chocolate-dipped ice cream cones.

While our parents were recording in the garage, Ben and I would ride our bikes through the front yard. Every afternoon at about three, our neighbor would come out onto the porch of his old Victorian house, sit in a chair facing the ocean, and play the violin. My brother and I would climb the kumquat tree to peer over the high walls. And there we'd sit, eating kumquats and watching the man perform.

After he finished, we'd climb back down and head out to the front yard and the beach to look for manatees, but we never saw any.

Once my mother had fully recovered, we all returned to California and the house we had left behind.

Our house in Hidden Hills, roughly 30 miles west of downtown Los Angeles, would become our genuine childhood home. My dad had located it for us. We lived there until I was twenty-one. It was a truly special spot, but it has since been demolished. There weren't many celebrities around back then. It was a horse community, and everyone owned one. My mother liked how far it was away. She appreciated how no celebrities lived there.

We had five acres. There was a swing in front of a massive ancient oak tree, fruit tree groves in the back, the main home, another large house, and two guesthouses. I recall going to visit the house for the first time, and the moment I saw the swing on the six-hundred-year-old oak tree, I knew I was sold.

The main house at Hidden Hills was rustic, featuring stone fireplaces and wood beams. Snakes would occasionally enter the home, and at night, we'd hear coyotes howl and great horned owls cry. Sometimes when I turned on the bathtub faucet, spiders would emerge. Tarantulas were commonly found in our backyard. I would bring them to school in jars for show-and-tell.

My mother's assistant and her kid live with us. He was our godbrother, and he, Ben, and I would simply roam. We were crashing motorcycles, running away, finding snakes, getting cut, and falling into rose bushes, much like my mother had done at Graceland. I believe we were protected by angels since none of us broke any bones, even when we fell off swings or crashed golf carts. My brother once flipped his golf buggy with off-road tires and decapitated it. He was somehow fine.

Along with the horses and seven dogs, we grew goats, chickens, and peacocks. Ben and I would spend hours, from sunup to dusk, playing in the orchards behind our house. We would imagine ourselves in our own worlds, making up games and spending hours in the trees playing make-believe.

We would climb the apple, plum, and pomegranate trees until we split open one and ate the mushy insides. Uant, my brother's nanny, would ring a bell at four o'clock for tea, crumpets, and jam, like a colonial British replica of her South African heritage. My mother handpicked everything for us; it was her idea of Graceland.

Aside from the Tarzana days with my father when things were easy, the decade following Michael Jackson was her best. She had a large number of friends that cared deeply for her. We would happily explore the world in a group of twenty-five persons. Fun all day, every day. I'd wake up to see a large group of folks enjoying coffee on the balcony. It was a dreamy communal existence. We were never alone. She was never alone.

Because my mother had witnessed Michael's life, we now had a private chef, three assistants, 10 security guards, agents, business managers, friends, and a slew of others coming and departing. At all times, the residences on the site were filled. Three of my friends moved in with me in the main house, and we even had my mother's holistic doctor living upstairs, as well as two nannies, for a total of roughly seventeen people, plus the individuals who came by every day. On her 2005 album Now What, she created a song, "Thanx," about those buddies.

One day, one tombstone.

All of our names should vanish. We share a life.

The beauty and ugliness

Despite all the misery and death

Birth of a child.

My mother has a Gaia-like quality, a mysterious intuition. Sometimes it felt as if Mother Nature was living through her.

One morning, my mother and father were drinking coffee in the kitchen when two of her friends, Mike and Caroline (who she had set up and who were now married and living with us in the top house), walked in.

"You're pregnant," my mother told Caroline.

Mike and Caroline turned white. Caroline was pregnant for only a few weeks. And they hadn't informed anyone.

I was talking about past incarnations as early as eleven years old; I felt that I had lived them and could recall them at one point, but I no longer do. I wished I could. I believe we have lived before, and the memories I have are related to how I died in a previous life.

I recall telling people when I was younger that I was riding a horse and buggy or in a carriage in an era before automobiles. They always thought I was insane when I stated it, but I did not train my own children to think that way. My kids would say the most outrageous things as young as three years old, and I'd just answer, "Really? That's cool!" I never wanted to remark, "That doesn't happen," "That's not possible," or "You don't know that." I never felt compelled to tear them down, as I did when I was younger.

My parents both wanted us to think the world was magical.

My mother would hire a Santa Claus to run through our yard on Christmas Eve, while my father would take us fairy hunting in the forest. My mother's bathroom had a secret tiny garden attached. I always thought it looked like a fairy garden, so I told Ben that's what it was. "If you ask the fairies for presents," I joked, "they'll bring them." He used to enjoy playing with my Polly Pocket dolls and would request one everytime we visited my mother's secret, enchanted garden. I went to the toy store and grabbed him some, then tied them to the trees overnight. The next day, he raced in, and I said, "Look what the fairies brought you!"

As I grew older, I realized that having a younger sibling may be a burden. When I acquired my first AOL account, I was about eleven years old, and I would race up to my mother's computer to see whether I had received an email. One day, Ben approached me and said, "I have a magical potion for you to drink."

This was annoying for an eleven-year-old girl who was hoping to receive an email.

"Go away!" I'm preoccupied with my email!"

"But it's a magical potion," he explained.

"No, it's not."

"Yes, it is-it's going to make you fly!"

"No, Ben, it's not going to make me fly," I answered, even though I secretly believed I could.

I knew I was destroying the enchantment, and he was so kind, so I said, "Okay, I'll try your magic elixir, but it won't help me fly. Watch..."

I took a gulp and instantly regretted it.

Despite getting a mouthful of unpleasant liquid, I was able to question, "What is in my mouth?"

"It's my pee," he explained.

Then, as Ben predicted, I was flying down the stairs and the long hallway to my bathroom. Ben followed me and laughed in the doorway as I spat up his miraculous medicine and brushed my teeth with soap repeatedly.

I went and found my mother.

"Ben made me drink his pee!" I wailed.

"Benjamin..." she said, and that was all. He never actually got into trouble. All he'd ever heard was "Benjamin..." If he was truly in difficulty, "Benjamin Storm..."

Everyone loved him too much to be furious with him.

Another time, I pursued him into the laundry room and told him I didn't want to play with him since he was such an obnoxious younger brother. I recall having a VHS cassette in my hand and being so upset that I pulled it up high, as if I was going to beat him with it. He began sobbing.

I've felt awful about that my entire life. As I already stated, he may easily shatter my heart.

Because he was the most adorable young boy you could imagine.

We attended Lewis Carroll Private School in Woodland Hills, which is three stop signs down the road from our house. My mom would pick us up at the end of the day, but she wasn't very interested in our education. We didn't need to be sick; we could simply tell her we didn't want to go to school, and she'd say, "Great! "You are staying at home and hanging out with me." Even on the way to school, Ben and I would explain to her why we needed to stay home that day, and as we approached the school, she'd turn the car around and drive back out, and we'd end up eating ice cream or going to the toy store.

My father, on the other hand, insisted that we receive an education, follow a routine, and have structure. But my mother was in charge, and she got her way. My mother allowed my father to homeschool us at one point. I only recall him telling us about ancient Egypt. How Orion's Belt connected with the Great Pyramids. To this day, I wow people more with my knowledge of constellations than with my arithmetic skills.

Priscilla gave birth to her second kid, a boy named Navarone, a few years before I arrived. Priscilla was a new mom again, and my mother was a new mom, so they spent a lot of time together because they both had young children. It became a point of agreement between them, a new beginning, a burying of the hatchet—though I know my mother was a little envious of Navarone, too, because here was this young kid whom Priscilla adored.

Priscilla's mother, Nana, was the matriarch of our family and the ultimate grandmother. Nona (Priscilla) did not fit the stereotype of a "granny," but Nana certainly did. Every Sunday, the entire extended family gathered for dinner at Nana's house in Brentwood. She created outstanding burnt baked potatoes, which we would eat with salad in the potato skins. Sometimes she'd make us pasta and serve it with cottage cheese. In fact, my mother would never eat spaghetti without cottage cheese; she claimed it was a "Beaulieu thing," referring to Priscilla's maiden name. After dinner, my grandma would always serve Push Pops for the kids.

I felt fortunate that we had such a large family and so many cousins. I had a large number of cousins--perhaps twenty in total--and we had the nicest time for many years, with plenty of fun and joy, and numerous visits to Hawaii--a normal family, albeit famous.

We'd spend most Thanksgivings at Nana's, and we'd frequently visit her house at Lake Arrowhead during the holidays, where we'd run wild outside, climbing boulders and digging for arrowheads while the adults drank wine and watched movies.

Nona would routinely pick me up or drop me off at her place, like my mother did. I probably saw Nona at least once a week. We spent every holiday, Christmas, and Sunday together. I was vaguely aware that my mother and her mother had had serious disagreements when my mother was younger, yet a peek at family photo albums or home films reveals a really tight family.

Later, in our teen years, Navarone and I attended the same school, so I frequently slept over at my grandmother's house so that we could travel to and from school together--he and I grew close.

I didn't know the entire extent of my mother's relationship with her mother until much later. For a long time, they let the past be the past, allowing Priscilla to remain our grandmother. From my perspective, we were a tight, regular family. Those Sunday dinners at Nona's continued far into my adulthood.

For two decades, our family felt pretty normal to me.

When I was younger, my mother would take me everywhere she went. I recall her doing a picture session in New York with Kevyn Aucoin. He dressed her up to look like Marilyn Monroe; I couldn't believe how stunning she was and how much she resembled her. Kevyn also handled my makeup after he finished with my mother; I remember his loud voice and large hands. She would take me to Cartier photo shoots, Vogue photo shoots, and even a fitting with Donatella Versace. While my mother tried on outfits, I roamed about the studio with Donatella's daughter, Allegra. When we left that day, my mother carried an incredible, very heavy, sequined Versace gown. I'm not sure how often she wore it, but I always enjoyed looking through her closet. It was wonderful for me.

One of my favorite things to do was sneak into my mother's enormous closet while she wasn't around and try on her gowns. She loathed it when I took her belongings. When I was thirteen, I snuck in and grabbed one of her favorite bags, a black Chanel purse with a gold diamond eagle on it. I was heading to Six Flags with some pals and thought it would be cool to take the purse. But during a break between roller coasters, I placed the bag on the bench behind me, and when I rose up to leave, it was gone.

That was the one secret I ever concealed from my mother when I was growing up. I finally told her when I was about twenty. I don't think she could recall which Chanel purse it was because she had so many.

I would frequently find myself at gatherings with her. When I was about nine years old, my mother took me to a party at Alanis Morissette's beach house in Malibu. My mother didn't know anyone at the party; she didn't go out of her way to make friends because she was naturally timid, so I became her friend for the night, as was typical.

We eventually found some vegan food--I recall there was a lot of vegan food--and spent the rest of the night alone by a campfire on the beach, chatting. Through the darkness, we noticed two adults rolling around on the sand making out. My mother hid my eyes.

"Don't look," she replied.

When my mother went to parties in the Hollywood Hills, if she saw someone she felt I would like to meet, she would call me out of bed in the middle of the night and ask me to come to wherever she was.

Someone came in one night after I had gone to bed and handed me a phone.

"I'm at a party," she told me, "and you'll never believe who's here!"

"Who?" I spoke groggily.

"Marilyn Manson!" Would you like to come meet him?"

At the time, I was a huge Manson fan. So, despite the fact that it was a school night and an hour trip from Hidden Hills to Hollywood Hills, security drove me to Jacqui Getty's house for the party. I met Marilyn Manson and then walked upstairs with some other kids. We spent the entire night trying on wigs until the adults were done.

Much later, on my sixteenth birthday, when I was deep into a Led Zeppelin period and had gotten a ZoSo tattoo, my mother called me from Peppone's in Brentwood. "Let's have dinner for your birthday!" she told me. Again, security pulled me over. I met my mother in the parking lot, and when we entered the restaurant, Robert Plant was there waiting for us.

Most evenings, I would fall asleep to the sounds of a party, with the piano being played and people singing loudly. Ben and I would sometimes sleep together in the same bed, which was quite reassuring for us. My mother had other relationships, but my father stayed in the guesthouse.

My mother's routine was the same every night she was home: a massage while watching Nick at Nite. Then she would come and lie with us and sing us lullabies like Mama's little baby likes shortnin', shortnin'.... or Lullaby and good night, Mommy and Daddy love you. That's generally where that song stops, but Mom would keep going, mentioning every single person and animal we'd ever met, until we went asleep: "Grandma Janet loves you, Nona loves you, Idy and Aunt love you, all the dogs-Oswald, Ruckus, Lulu, Winston, Puffy love you...."

Or maybe my father would read us The Hobbit. Then they'd both say good night, sometimes a little tipsy and wild, in which case our nannies would sit with us until the sound of coyotes drew me into a dream I'd always had, a place where nothing bad ever happened and we all lived forever in each other's orbits, the closest family you could imagine.

My mother considered holidays to be really important. On Christmas morning, we would see puppies creeping out of stockings. We used to get newborn chicks and bunnies for Easter.

For her birthdays, she would rent out a portion of Magic Mountain, just like her father had done with Libertyland in Memphis. She enjoyed roller coasters. Zippin Pippin was the first roller coaster she fell in love with, so for her birthday, she hired Colossus and went on it approximately seven hundred times in a row all night with me and Ben. She insisted on riding with her security guards until the lights turned green.

We'd have large Thanksgiving feasts, with everyone dressed up. There was nothing low-key. She wished that every moment was special.

But then there were evenings when I walked into her room and found her alone, crying while listening to her father's music on the floor.

My mother found it difficult to pursue a profession in music. She was a lovely lyricist, but she didn't believe she had complete control over her music. I thought it was very bold of her to make a record at all.

After a day in the studio, she'd summon me and my brother to sit in her Mercedes and listen to the song she'd recorded that day. She would play it for us loudly, and we would tell her what we thought. And if we weren't at school because we skipped class or it was the weekend, we'd accompany her to the studio--there was even a song she wrote about us, "So Lovely," that we got to perform on:

You know I did something correctly!

Something that keeps me alive

Oh, you darling tiny babies!

When you arrived, you explained why I was finally satisfied.

Did you know me before now?

My God, you're so wonderful!

Did you come here to help me? I know you can't sleep well unless I'm right next to you. You also take care of Mommy. You're fast to defend me.

Please don't be afraid to lose me.

You know, I have the same anxieties.

My mother enjoyed touring, but it wasn't profitable for her because she wasn't giving people what they expected, which was for her to sing Elvis songs. Elvis impersonators would appear at her gigs. She'd always dreaded that. She would peek out the edge of the curtain before each act to see if any impersonators were in the audience so she could prepare. It's strange to have someone see you sing while dressed up as your late father. She desperately wanted to be taken seriously, but it seemed unlikely.

Despite the Elvis impersonators, my mother enjoyed the tour experience. We enjoyed it as well--we'd travel on the tour bus with her, sleeping in bunk beds, going from city to city, in and out of motels to shower, and then on to another town, another Cracker Barrel and Waffle House, sound check, nap, and play the concert. She enjoyed discovering local bars, playing, and then hanging out. She would occasionally invite fans to join us in the greenroom after a show.

I enjoyed performing live because of the rapid response and the chance to interact with the crowd. You're typically alone in the studio, but when I performed live, I could observe people's faces and see how my words or music impacted them. I could always tell by the look on their faces. And then meeting the fans and hearing them tell me how much my music had helped them was incredible.

I also thoroughly loved communicating with both my own and my father's admirers. I would do everything in my power, almost to the point of exhaustion. I'd do everything they requested, including talking to them and taking pictures. I used to spend a lot of time doing it on the road. I've always thought it was vital to be gracious and thankful.

My music can be somber, dark, lonely, and dismal. But after the shows, individuals tell me that the songs saved their lives because they could relate—they, too, have been in that position and experienced that life. I've had so many individuals come backstage and tell me that, even though what I perform is gloomy, it has literally kept them from committing themselves. Oh my God, is anyone else feeling this way? I adore it when they tell me that. It encourages me to keep doing it.

I sensed the weight of the business from her debut hit, "Lights Out." Every time the record business gave it to her for approval, it became more country-oriented, catering to Elvis fans. I recall sitting in her Mercedes, saying, "I liked the original version, but I really don't like this...." The corporation refused to give her what she wanted, and she refused to give them what they wanted.

I don't like performing Elvis songs, but I'd try to do something special for the fans on his death anniversary, especially if it was a significant year. I recorded a duet with him called "Don't Cry Daddy" in 1997 as a surprise for the fans, and then again a few times after that. These performances were not included on any record or anything I sold (save for charity once). On the one hand, I feel like my performance of his songs was a touch cheesy, but on the other, I enjoy having my own personality as much as I can.

In 2013, when I performed at Graceland, we played three tracks from my Storm & Grace CD in the Jungle Room. I recall feeling at ease because it was my home, but I also became quite concerned about all of the people in there, as well as the wear and tear on the situation. The carpets are just stunning.

During the production of her second album, Now What, she would come home and tell us what each song was about. She recorded the Ramones song "Here Today, Gone Tomorrow" for Johnny Ramone, a close friend who died a year before. "When You Go" is half about myself and half about my father.

But one song, "High Enough," jumps out right now. She wasn't doing drugs at the time, but she was drinking—some nights far too much—

and the song is plainly about addiction. But this was far before any of us could have predicted it would become such a problem for her, though storm clouds were forming even then.

My mother met Nicolas Cage in October 2000 during Johnny Ramone's birthday party, and they married in Hawaii on August 10, 2002. I was thirteen years old. When she met Nic, she had been in a serious relationship with musician John Oszajca for two years.

She and John were madly in love and had been engaged for a time, but he was six years younger than her, and the fact that she had children and an ex-husband who was still very much in her life made things difficult for them. They eventually split up, and she constantly wondered what might have happened if they hadn't.

Crazy things kept happening. There were other attempts to poison the well with my father, for example—people connected to my grandmother informed my mother that Danny had been selling her out to the press.

To prove that, they had a PI on my father for months. He was once playing blackjack for money in Las Vegas, and the PI followed him. Then my father received a call from two of his friends, Cyndi Lauper and Angela McCluskey, asking him to meet them at Sundance, and despite the fact that he was prone to wearing a top hat and limping around with a cane after injuring his leg on a motorcycle, the PI still managed to lose him and informed my mother that they had no idea where he was.

"He stole a car and ran away," the PI stated.

My father met Cyndi and Angela at Sundance, when they all attended a party for the French band Air. And whom did Danny meet at the party? My mother, her boyfriend, and her chief of security.

Danny said, "Hi!" when he spotted my mother.

My mom's jaw fell. Her private investigator had lost my father, but he had found my mother, as he always did.

My mother's romance with Nic Cage lasted only briefly. It felt like something came in and then disappeared, like a Florida storm, and I believe it served as a distraction from her separation with John. She even alternated between Nic and John for a minute. I recall coming into her room one day and seeing Nic, and the next day John. She obviously couldn't make up her mind.

But Nic and my mom had a great day together. I'm not sure if they were actually in love, though she claimed they were. He'd bring her diamonds, and every time he came to see her, he'd be in a different car--usually a Lamborghini and always in a different color (I recall a green, an orange, and a red one, but never the same car again). My brother, who was seven years old when they met, couldn't quite pronounce it correctly. He'd say, "Here's Nic in his Lamborghini."

Nic got my mother two gorgeous old cars: a 1959 blue Corvette convertible and a 1960s white Cadillac. My mother would take me and Ben to school in the morning. I preferred the Corvette because I enjoy riding with the top down.

On weekends, we'd all board a yacht and cruise to Catalina Island off the southwestern coast of Los Angeles. During one of these visits, she and Nic had a dispute, and her $65,000 engagement ring wound up in the ocean. (She claimed in a subsequent Diane Sawyer interview that it was worth more, and that she did not toss it, but that it was thrown....) A diver was promptly dispatched to locate it, but there was no hope because the water between Catalina and Los Angeles is 3,000 feet deep.

Nic got her another ring, this one even more expensive than the first.

On that yacht, I first saw the film Jaws. My mother forced my brother and me to watch it; she enjoyed horror films, especially those set in a frightful atmosphere. So we saw Jaws on a yacht in the middle of the ocean, Misery while locked up in a ski lodge in Jackson Hole, The Ring in Japan, and Black Christmas on Christmas Eve stuck in a cabin on Lake Arrowhead. She and my brother adored it, screaming and laughing throughout, even though it was never my thing. In fact, I was thoroughly traumatized.

It did not stop with movies. My mother came up at school dressed as Michael Myers from the Halloween movie. Another time, she appeared as a bloodied and dead Marie Antoinette. We got back at her, though: Ben and I would take turns donning the Michael Myers mask and chasing each other and her around the house. She would be more terrified than anyone.

After 108 days, her turbulent marriage to Nic Cage was over. In that interview with Diane Sawyer, my mother stated about the relationship, "We were so dramatic, the two of us, that we couldn't stay contained."

For the most of my life, my mother maintained a residence on Hawaii's Big Island and spent as much time there as possible. She stated that she felt connected to the island and could think more clearly there.

As I previously stated, my mother always made birthdays and holidays a big thing, so for my sixteenth birthday, a huge group of us traveled to Hawaii: myself and six of my closest friends, Ben and two of his friends, my mother and several of her friends, her future husband Michael Lockwood, and my father.

My mother hosted a great celebration for me on the beach, with a person singing and playing guitar as we ate. My father gave me sixteen presents. At some time, he requested me and my father to join him on the grass dance floor for a father-daughter dance. My father and I exchanged terrified looks (thank goodness he was at least four mai tais in, or it would have been an even worse nightmare). We were anxious to get out of it, but my mother insisted since she thought it would be amusing.

The song he chose to accompany the dance was Bob Carlisle's "Butterfly Kisses," about a daughter being sent from heaven to be daddy's little girl, one part lady, and looking more like her mama by the day. Nothing against the song, but putting my family members in a traditional environment was always going to go poorly. We found the entire thing hilarious, and my father and I simply clutched each other, convulsing with laughter. Everyone at the table cracked up. My father, like Ben, has a fantastic chuckle that makes it impossible not to laugh along with him--truthfully, that dance was the hardest I've ever laughed in my life, and not just because my friends and I had been stealing our own mai tais and champagne all night.

At the end of the party, we returned to the house in golf carts to listen to music and continue partying. My mother always had her own bottle of Dom Pérignon, which no one was allowed to touch. She enjoyed dancing to seventies music, such as Sister Sledge's "We Are

Family" and Van McCoy's "The Hustle," during which she forced everyone to perform the actual hustle. She typically only wanted to blast disco...and Britney Spears' "Toxic."

She took hip-hop dance classes at our Hidden Hills home. (She made me do it, too, but I wasn't very good.) She had me do everything with her; at some time, she had learned a dance to TLC's "Creep," and when she dropped me off at a sleepover in the Valley, she stayed to teach me and my friends the movements. She would frequently hang out with us. She would respond, "Your friends are my friends."

"Maggie May" came on at some point that night in Hawaii, and we all shouted along, with some dancing on tables till the early hours.

Around three a.m. I took a break by lying on a lawn chair and gazing at the stars. Shooting stars are common in Hawaii, and they were rushing by my peripheral vision. My mother came to join me, and we lay there together, watching the streaking lights.

I replied, "My stomach hurts."

She responded: "That's because you've been drinking my Dom Pérignon."

We eventually discovered that someone was missing. We had somehow lost my father on the five-minute drive from the beach to the house. This was not unusual when we were partying because he was always the wildcard. But I was anxious, so Ben and his friend went back out to get him; they returned without my father but with a big toad they had discovered.

My mother never worried about my father. "He'll outlive us all," she'd say.

During the dancing celebration, I spotted a figure in the distance approaching our backyard, emerging from the massive, jagged lava rock behind our house.

My father was shirtless, with a small dot of blood on his nose. No one knew how he got through the lava or what he was doing out there. This was not uncommon for Danny. He would simply show up with a mischievous smile on his face, as if nothing had occurred. But everything had happened.

The night went on like so many others, with my parents dancing together and laughing in their own world. They always reminded me of a pair of pirates.

As I prepared to go to bed (I could never stay as long as my parents), I discovered that my father had removed the remainder of his clothes and was now sitting naked in a lawn chair, peacefully drinking champagne with my mother's security guards.

My mother badly wanted a regular life, and Michael Lockwood felt like her final chance. It appeared that in Michael, she had found someone who could help her stop running from stability.

As my mother began to explore marrying again, she reconsidered her connection with her own mother, and they got closer, not just for the sake of me and my brother, but for themselves. To attempt to heal what had been done. My mother wrote the song "Raven" for Priscilla:

I will hear your stories.

That filled your sorrowful eyes when you had raven hair.

Hold your head up high.

I know I have been ruthless.

I have been ruthless

Go ahead, dry your eyes...

Hey, you finally see me!

Hi

And I see you!

And everything until now.

It wasn't all that horrible, Beautiful lady.

Go ahead, dry your eyes.

You are aware that I have forgiven you, and I apologize.

And everything until now.

It wasn't too horrible.

Beautiful gal.

My mother wanted to forgive her. She also wanted to accept responsibility for her role in their troubled relationship. Those lines meant the world to her mother. After that, Nona would come on tour and be overjoyed to hear her music. For a brief while, my grandmother and mother were as close as can be. They were often grinning and laughing, having fun and getting drunk together, and generally getting into trouble.

In 2005, my mother and Michael got engaged in Hawaii. I recall her returning to our house in Hidden Hills and showing me the ring in the kitchen.

My mother loved Japan and its culture, and she wanted a traditional Japanese wedding, so they married in Kyoto in January 2006.

Approximately twenty of us traveled to Japan for the event. I was two days late because I had stomach flu. My father, who would be the best man at the wedding, waited and then flew with me to Tokyo.

From Tokyo, we all rode the train to Kyoto and stayed in a traditional ryokan. The day after I arrived in Kyoto, my mother and I had the traditional Japanese breakfast of fish, miso soup, and rice, but I ordered a side of white bread and jam because I'd never seen such a fluffy slice of bread in my life. After breakfast, my closest friend and I went with my mom and her mom to a clothing shop to get measured for traditional wedding kimonos.

At the rehearsal dinner, my mother motioned for me to join her outdoors. We headed off together, smoking cigarettes, down a beautiful old little lane (as is the case with most Kyoto roads).

During the trip, my mother said, "I'm having a panic attack in there, I don't know why...." We walked a little further, and she said, "I felt stuck at that table. I needed to go outside." I was only sixteen at the time, and I had no idea what was going on, though I suspected she was terrified of commitment. Perhaps she was aware that this was the beginning of the final chapter.

Nevertheless, the next day, my mother married in the ryokan's backyard. I will never forget how stunning she looked. After the wedding, we rode the train to Hakone and the Gora Kadan hot springs, which are located on the grounds of Kan'in-no-miya residence, a former summer residence of an imperial family member.

This was one of my mother's favorite spots on the planet. She adored the hotel and the hot springs. I remember the two of us cleaning our bodies while sitting on small stools before entering the tubs. We did not say anything. I believe we were both just taking in the beauty around us and feeling grateful to be there and with each other.

Later that night, in our kimonos, we headed down to the hotel's karaoke bar, the one location on the property where it's acceptable to let loose a little bit--in fact, I think it's encouraged. Michael Lockwood sang David Bowie's "Let's Dance," my father sang the Troggs' "Wild Thing," my mother and I sang Elton John's "Your Song," and then I sang two ABBA songs with my best friend, my mother joining in with "Chiquitita," until the three of us ended up crying on the floor from laughing so hard.

By the end of the night, my father was dancing with Priscilla, my brother was racing around with a friend, and my mother and I were dancing with the natives, as you do.

My mother urgently wanted more children. She went through several rounds of IVF and eventually became pregnant.

During her pregnancy with my sisters, mother rented a house in Montecito as the first chapter of a fairy-tale existence she envisioned for herself and her new offspring. She was out of L.A., it was a lovely summer, and we would

Spend these lovely days enjoying her pregnancy in her calm garden.

My mother had a profound spiritual intuition about the two beings inside her. She imagined Harper as delicate, feminine, and strong, and Finley as spunky, stubborn, and sweet. And she was correct. That is who they are.

My mother was like a hurricane. However, everyone observes how sweet and kind her children are.

In October 2008, she gave birth to twin daughters: Harper Vivienne Ann Lockwood, named after Michael's mother and Priscilla, and Finley Aaron Love Lockwood, named after Gladys and Elvis.

Harper and Finley were the loveliest little newborns. They were born via C-section at Los Robles Hospital in Thousand Oaks.

I, along with Michael Lockwood, were present when my mother had her C-section. When they came out, I recall thinking they looked exactly how we expected. They both had Cupid's bow lips and heavy eyelids, as we all have.

I was nineteen, and they felt like my babies, too.

After my mother's C-section, it was critical to get her up and moving as soon as possible, so we'd walk the hospital corridors together, holding on to her small walker. She disliked doing it, but to cheer her up, I'd speak to her in this strange language she, Ben, and I had invented when we were kids. (She had a similar experience with her father.) If we truly wanted to, we could speak that language and no one else would understand us. Every day I'd walk into her bed, she'd be cranky and in pain, and I'd say, "Do you want to stroll the Isles of Robles?" And we'd leave, laughing hysterically.

When the twins arrived home, we all started about feeding and burping these two angels. Their father would feed one, my mother would feed the other, and I'd be on burping duty (I normally slept on a cot in the room).

I like getting up at night with the babies. We were all quite close. If we were in a hotel, my sisters would sleep in bed with my mother, while I would sleep on a cot at their feet. We were constantly in the same room together.

My mother was extremely intuitive and instinctive when it came to becoming a mother. She could see right away that Finley preferred to be held this manner, as did Harper. I'm not sure where she got it--I don't think it was something she inherited; instead, I believe she was born that way. Circumstances change a person, but there's a part of you that is your spirit, and my mother's spirit was full of maternal love.

For years, she wished for another chance to be a mother. She had been a young mother with Ben and I, and she wanted to do it again, this time with more thought and more time with her children. She did not want a large crew of nannies to raise them. She wanted to handle everything herself, hands on.

Ben and I had wonderful, amazing childhoods, but my mother still wanted to do a better job the second time around, to be more present and do everything herself. So she devised a plan: she was going to sell Los Angeles. house and move to England to live a nice rural life with my sisters, who would have a country garden and go for walks every morning, growing up with cute British accents.

This is one of the most tragic aspects of the last decade of her life: becoming a mother was the most important thing to her, and she had hoped for another opportunity at it, but her addiction intervened.

Her father had been an addict, but there was little understanding of this in the 1970s. Back then, everyone in Hollywood appeared to be an addict, but no one had a word for it. Elvis had assumed he was simply following his physicians' orders--if the doctor told him to take a medicine to fall asleep and another to wake up, he complied. His motives were pure. So my mother's addiction may have had a genetic component; in any case, it waited until shortly after my sisters were born.

Then it appeared and burned everything down.

My mother's life quickly became out of control. She had so many employees running everything for her that she didn't know how to turn on the living room television. She'd had a fantastic run, a decade of allowing people in and trusting them. However, money was a component of her life that she was largely unaware of. One day she learned that a certain employee had perhaps misused the business credit card. She started looking into it and discovered that some employees were overcharging her cards in ways she didn't approve of--too many flights, too many new phones, and too many pizzas. Most of these co-workers were also her closest friends. They weren't thieves; perhaps they just became a little sluggish. However, it alleviated my mother's long-held suspicion that everyone around her had a hidden goal. Even deeper, she believed she was unlovable. She dealt with these emotions by excluding people, no matter how serious the infraction.

At the end of that idyllic 10 years, my mother abruptly fired everyone at Hidden Hills, including friends, security, assistants, and people she had known and loved for years. Her religion. She just wanted everything gone.

They were sent away one by one. The only people left were her children, Michael Lockwood, and, of course, my father.

Something in her heart had never left Graceland and had not emotionally evolved since her father's death. She told herself how much she wanted friends, but after nearly forty years of constant disappointments--people selling her out to the press, being careless with her money, dating her for the wrong reasons--she learned to cut people out of her life without looking back.

For the first time in her life, she wished to be alone.

She left the house alone one day, which she had never done before, and went to a little indie cinema in Woodland Hills to see any movie she could find, which happened to be Into the Wild. She knew nothing about the film ahead of time. My mother's first solo activity was watching that movie. I was frightened, but I also remember thinking, What a fortunate film to have stumbled across: a picture about a young, idealistic man venturing out into the forest on his own, discovering his identity through solitude.

However, it ends tragically.

I can be quite rude and aggressive, and it freaks others off. It stems from attempting to shield myself from pain. I just push people away. It's the dread of getting wounded. I know people can injure me, therefore I'll keep them out.

I learned from the finest, Michael Jackson. He did it exceptionally well.

But, even as a child, I recall being very upset with my aunt and saying, "I disown you; don't ever talk to me again." My aunt! I'm really sensitive, fearful, and insecure about who I am. I'm not sure who I am; I never had the chance to discover my own identity. I did not have a family. I did not have a childhood, and while some of it was enjoyable, there was also continual trouble.

And suddenly I awoke. I became aware of a number of events that had occurred around me throughout the years. Many individuals were invested in keeping me quiet and manageable.

By then, unbeknownst to us all, she was frequently taking the opioids prescribed to her following the C-section she had for my sister's delivery.

Chapter 7: The Bus From Nashville To L.A.

If you don't have something to keep you focused, or some kind of purpose, it's hard out there. Life is not easy. Who doesn't want to be high? Drugs or drinking make you feel great.

You have to have something bigger, bigger than that feeling of being high, bigger than that happiness, bigger than that emptiness. If you don't, you're in trouble.

Before I became addicted, I was focused. I wanted to know what the fuck I was doing here, I wanted to know about life, I wanted to know about people. For a long time,

I didn't want to fuck around. I needed answers, whatever they were. That had been my focus.

But as soon as that was gone, I was off the rails. When I had my twins and I was in the hospital and they gave me Norco, that's when I felt the first oh-my-God high from a painkiller.

I was forty.

I don't really know what I was doing, to be honest. I was getting isolated, slowly starting to get rid of everyone and everything in my life, all the pillars I had set up, all the people and the friends and the relationships. I was starting to, one by one, dislodge and dismantle each and every one of those things.

My mother had started by taking opioids for pain after her C-section, and then she progressed to taking them to sleep.

She had turned forty in February 2008; my sisters were born in October that same year (I would turn twenty the following May). After her brief stint with drugs as a teenager she had never touched them again. She drank, but, like she said, as an adult she wouldn't even take Advil or Tylenol.

Throughout my life she would often say, "If I tried drugs, it would be over for me." I see now that that was such a strong hint to an addiction issue she had an intuition about. I think it was subconscious, but it stalked her. She had been holding it back with Scientology, with raising children, with marriages, with spirituality.

But it was there, like a shadow, the whole time. She'd say, "My dad was forty-two when he died. I'm thirty-nine...."

We never could have imagined it would be something that would come for her so viciously, so late in life.

Shortly after my sisters were born, to try to gain some agency, my mom moved with them and Michael Lockwood to England.

Initially, they lived briefly in southwest London, Richmond, and some days she would take my sisters in their stroller to a little crepe restaurant on the Thames. My mom loved the quaint life she was creating for herself.

Ben and I felt a bit abandoned because her move to England meant that for the first time we didn't all live together in the same house. She got us a house in Calabasas, but we pretty much stayed in England with her most of the time.

My mom had originally thought about living in Ireland -we would go to Ireland a lot when we were younger. My mom was friends with the Austrian-Irish artist Gottfried Helnwein, and we'd stay at his castle, Castle Gurteen de La Poer, in Kilsheelan, a few miles east of Clonmel. We'd all go to the local pubs and dance to the music, and then when closing time came, we'd head back to Gurteen and run around the castle grounds, or climb a spiral tower to the top and lay under the stars, me drunk at seventeen, until the sun peered through the crenellations.

So my mom had really wanted to move to Ireland, but every property she found she claimed was haunted. She had a very practical and pragmatic connection to ghosts, past lives, and spirits. One day a realtor took us to a very old house somewhere outside of Cork. She led us down a hallway with pink floral wallpaper and a very low ceiling. Before we even reached the living room, my mom said, "It's haunted," turned around, and walked right out.

She soon settled in England instead. In the beginning, England, like Hidden Hills before it, was really magical— the first couple of years especially. It seemed to me that she thought this was her last shot at stability, once more having children and living in a huge country house in the middle of nowhere. Again she was trying to recreate what she had felt with my father. A simple life without all of the people. Just her husband and her children.

After Richmond, in 2010, she bought a fifteenth-century property in Rotherfield, about thirty miles northeast of Brighton on the south coast. The house had fifty acres, a gorgeous lake, sheep, horses, topiary, even an orangery-it was truly beautiful, stunning.

It was also haunted, but only in one room. Finley told my mother and Michael that she often saw a man in her bedroom. Eventually my mother and Michael got more details: Apparently, the great-grandmother of a resident of the house had lived-and died-in the house. And the loud bangs that they all regularly heard around midnight were probably to do with the great-grandfather who had shot himself in the barn many years earlier-the same barn that was now their living room.

My mom got very into gardening in England. She would plant radishes, potatoes, and carrots in the garden with my sisters. It was also the first time she cooked-she still had a chef, but she had more time on her hands so spent some of it in the kitchen. We would take tea by the fire all day, too— she loved making and stoking fires. She would just sit there and intently watch the flames, trying to predict them. No one could make a fire blaze like my mother-she was a fire witch.

Every weekend Ben and I would take the train up to London to meet up with our friends. At Christmastime wed head to Harrods in Knightsbridge or to the Borough Market in Southwark, do our Christmas shopping, then head back to our local pub in Crowborough, a few miles from the house, to hang out with the locals and sing and dance till the wee hours of the morning. (By this time my mom had become close friends with the owners of the pub so we could skirt the eleven P.M. closing bell and staying up all night.) Ben was eighteen and sometimes he'd work behind the bar.

This was my mom's idea of living a small life—she still had a house manager, one security guard, one driver, a chef, and two nannies for the girls, which sounds like a lot, but was a skeleton crew compared to what had been going on in California. Eventually she'd create her own pub at the house, where a bunch of the locals, including some new friends like guitarist Jeff Beck, his wife Sandra, and Sarah Ferguson, could hang out. (Sarah and my mom had a real loyalty toward each other-they'd both been through similar onslaughts in the press and in life, torn apart and shamed simply for being women who were unapologetically themselves.) And my mom had huge Christmas parties, too. Mostly, though, she liked going to the chip shop and having a roast on Sundays and gardening with my sisters.

Seemingly she had done what she set out to do: She had created a very sweet little life in the countryside. So the first couple years were truly magical.

We had no idea, though, that her pill use was very slowly increasing.

One night we all went up to London to hang out at Soho House. Typically, when my mother and I got into fights they would resolve themselves fairly quickly. She could be rational, could take responsibility, and be empathetic. That night at Soho House, though, was the first time I realized something was wrong.

It began as a small argument about me wanting to go to Ireland before Christmas, but quickly I felt a viciousness from her I had never felt before. She wouldn't resolve the argument, and the back-and-forth felt very irrational.

"You didn't tell me you were going to Ireland this close to Christmas," she said.

"Yes, I did tell you," I said, "you just don't remember." She ignored that.

"So, you're going to leave me here and take your brother to Ireland? That's just so not right, so it's not okay to do that."

"I just told you: I told you weeks ago we were going to Ireland. I'm so confused right now...."

She became relentless; she wouldn't let it go. There was a new meanness in her where before we would have resolved it quickly.

I was so confused and angry at the exchange that I stormed out of the club. It made me feel crazy. On my way out I found my brother having a cigarette.

"Mom is being so weird...." I said.

"What do you mean?" he said.

"Like, she's just getting mad that we're going to Ireland when we already told her weeks ago. She won't let it go."

I was dressed in a fancy gown, and I had nowhere to go -it was two A.M. As I walked away, a rickshaw passed me, and I got in. The rickshaw was all decked out in Christmas lights, and the guy was blasting "Angels" by Robbie Williams so loud I couldn't hear myself think. There I was, dressed in a floor-length gown and faux fur coat, and even in my fury I couldn't help but see the absurdity of the situation and laugh at myself. I texted my mom a video of me riding through Oxford Circus as the song blasted. My mother sent a text back: "Hah!" After fights, we wouldn't typically have a conversation to resolve the fight. Eventually one person would just break the silence and it was back to business as usual this was that text. I headed back to Soho House.

But things were changing. And not just with my mom.

After a couple of years of living in England, we all went to Hawaii on vacation, and that's when my mom admitted to me that yes, she was addicted to opioids, but that she was planning on going to rehab in Mexico. Me and my brother and sisters went to Mexico with her. Halfway through, though, she made an excuse to cut it short.

"I'm going to have to go back-the girls are starting school after Easter," she said.

"What do you mean?" I said. "Surely you knew this was landing on those dates?"

"Yeah, but they just started. They have all these new friends. They have their routine. I'm not going to pull them out of that...."

"I think everyone would agree that you staying here is more important than my sisters missing a week of school," I said, but she was adamant. She always did what she wanted to do. My brother and I were angry, but we couldn't change her mind.

Back in England, there was a tacit awareness between me, my brother, and Michael that maybe my mother didn't want to get sober. She was always extremely honest, but I think she felt that being honest was the virtue rather than the changing of her behavior. Since she had admitted it to us, honesty seemed to give her the license to continue with her addiction.

Now that we knew, my brother and I noticed things, like she would fall asleep too early when we watched movies together.

One morning I was sitting in the kitchen drinking tea, and as my mom came by, she slightly bumped into the wall as she passed. I felt a sense of dread because I knew from her telling me for years and years that if she ever did heroin, it would kill her. She would say, "I would never just dabble; if I did it, it would take me out."

Eventually she realized that moving to England hadn't been such a good idea. She had distanced herself from all of her friends, and the drug use had increased along with the loneliness and isolation. Or she needed to be alone to take the drugs. Or both.

Her community was gone. She was in the English countryside with two babies and no friends. She decided that isolation was the problem. She hated L.A. and wanted to be closer to Graceland, so she decided she was going to move to Nashville to be more social, and make a new record.

I felt better. This felt like she had a plan. Danny was going to try to sell the house in England, and she was going to get off the pills and start over in Nashville.

While she looked for Nashville homes, she rented a house in L.A. on a golf course with a beautiful backyard, a pool, and a movie room where my brother and I would watch Game of Thrones.

One night I went downstairs to get a drink and I noticed that Michael was taking my sisters out of the house to Chuck E. Cheese. It was strange that my mom wasn't going with them. I went upstairs to find her and headed into her room. I realized that she was hiding in her bathroom.

"Don't come in," she said.

I ignored her.

When I entered, I found her crying in her bathtub. She had a black eye and a bloody nose-she'd fallen while high. She was sobbing and clearly felt ashamed. She'd told Michael to take my sisters out so that they wouldn't see her face.

She knew this had all gone too far. She went back to rehab the following week.

After that stint, she then flew to Nashville.

My mother was slowly falling apart. My brother was, too.

We were all drinking a lot, but even when he drank, my brother remained jovial, fun. He was somebody who never wanted the night to end, the last person awake.

But there was one night at a club when I was around twenty-two and Ben started pushing me to leave. It didn't feel right. He got me in a taxi and sent me back to the hotel where we were staying for the weekend. Only later did I realize he'd been doing drugs-probably Molly or coke-and he had wanted me out of there so he could do whatever he wanted without me finding out.

This became a theme in my family: They would do things behind my back. I was kind of the narc-my mom always said I was too harsh on Ben or too harsh on her, but I think it was simply that I was the only one who wasn't an addict-so I was the downer.

But I was getting concerned about Ben. One night around that time, he was drinking at the pub, came back late, and fell off his bed and chipped his front tooth. He cried in my mom's arms that night at the bottom of the stairs.

Still, he never really drank during the day. He was a binge drinker, going hard for a couple of weeks and then stopping for a long stretch. We spent a lot of time with him sober. I would worry about him at the moment, but then the following week or month he'd be fine, better than fine— drinking green juices and working out.

It didn't affect my relationship with him, but my mom's addiction meant she was simply not there emotionally a lot of the time.

When I started talking to a therapist, it was really nice to hear somebody talk back and say, "Hey, you're not fucked up," or "You need to stop shooting yourself in the foot."

I also attended group therapy and initially I really resisted it. But eventually I started getting close to people. I realized that they were all as fucked up as me.

I didn't love AA. You talk about drugs and alcohol all the time and it drives me fucking crazy. I agree that I am powerless over it and I believe that I could stop everything, but the pills were designed to addict you from within. Even if you only take them for two or three weeks straight, you're going to have some kind of blowback. Your body's going to withdraw.

But I don't think it's just physical. I believe that a body is just a body, and the spirit is ultimately inside of the physical shell, and I don't think chemicals have anything

to do with the spirit. They make a physical addiction to the body-but the root of the addiction comes from being really unhappy. That's a spiritual problem.

After I left Scientology, I started upping the pills. I thought, Oh my God, I've lost my religion and it's been my only pavement to walk on, my replacement family. Everything was gone, all my friends, everything.

I knew it was over.

And I was so devastated, I used the drugs as a coping mechanism.

Two weeks into her new life in Nashville my mother was back on opioids.

The addiction got worse. She was drinking more, taking more opioids. At one point she found an article that said cocaine can help people get off opioids, so she began to do cocaine to get off the opioids and then opioids to get off the cocaine. Her addiction would continue through all of the stints in rehab on the basis that she was always in severe and life-threatening withdrawals that no doctor could understand. She felt all of the doctors were too harsh. They wouldn't give her enough of what she needed, so she was "doing it herself."

It escalated to eighty pills a day.

It took more and more to get high, and I honestly don't know when your body decides it can't deal with it anymore. But it does decide that at some point.

I believe that we're all born innocent, and that everyone's nature is innately good, but they get fucked by their surroundings. And I believe that my brain is different, that I am an addict. Otherwise I wouldn't have had all those years in between being a stupid teenager to suddenly getting a drug habit at forty.

For a couple of years it was recreational and then it wasn't. It was an absolute matter of addiction, withdrawal in the big leagues. If I had fully run out of drugs, the severity of the withdrawal would have left me either in the hospital or dead. My blood shot up so high. pressure would

I just wanted to check out. It was too painful to be sober.

My whole life had blown up, it felt like one thing after another, and I could not take any more beatings.

My mom came up with all kinds of reasons why she didn't want to get off drugs, but I think one of the most poignant ones was her feeling of shame about becoming an addict with two young children. Her parenting standards were so high that I don't think she could ever truly get sober knowing what she had put my sisters through. The one thing that she had always really prided herself on was that she was a great mother. She said, "My music wasn't that successful, I didn't finish high school, I'm not beautiful, I'm not good enough- but I'm a great mother."

When she started to feel like she wasn't even that, she couldn't handle it, so she doubled down.

When she lived in Nashville, in the depths of her addiction, my mom would often drive the two hundred miles southwest to Graceland to sleep in her dad's bed. It seemed like the only place she found any comfort.

Often, she would take me, Ben, and my sisters upstairs to his room and we would all sleep in her dad's bed while there were tours going on downstairs. I wish this was a magical time in a magical family place. But the truth of it was, she was in the house desperate to feel protected, desperate to connect with her father. She would lie in his bed, lie on his floor, anything to feel some comfort. It was the feeling of going to church when all is lost and saying, "Please, Jesus, help me."

And every time she went, she'd point out an empty plot of grass where she would eventually be laid to rest, next to her father in the Meditation Garden.

When I was back in L.A., I got a call from my mother.

"There's something wrong with me. Physically," she said.

"You need to come to L.A.," I said. "We need to get you to a hospital."

I was really unhappy and my body was not doing well. Riley and Ben wanted to get me to a doctor-everyone wanted to get me to the doctor, but I wouldn't go to one in Nashville-so Riley sent Ben to get me because my assistant, Christy, had told her that a couple of times she thought I had gone, that I had looked dead on the bed.

Ben showed up and he, the girls, and I took a tour bus all the way from Nashville to L.A. We drove because I wanted to do cocaine the whole time and couldn't if I was on an airplane. I didn't think I could even get through airport security. The tour bus had six beds, a bedroom in the back, and a kitchen.

When we arrived in L.A., I went straight in to see the head of Cedars-Sinai. I was at thirty heartbeats per minute. I lay there scared to death.

My echocardiogram came back bad. I was literally losing my heart. My heart was dead, just in pieces.

When she arrived in L.A. from Nashville, Mom's head and face were twice their normal size. She went straight from the emergency room to the ICU-she was in heart failure. It was chaos, and in the midst of it, she told Michael Lockwood she was leaving him.

It took about a week for her to start to recover.

Once she was feeling a bit better, she was desperate to find somewhere safe, somewhere gated, to live. She repeatedly asked if we could find somewhere on Mountaingate, where we'd all lived when I was little, where we'd lost Jaco the pug but where we'd been so happy....

My mother had changed business management at that time and somehow all of her credit cards had been frozen. She had nothing. Everything was a mess. She went to court-ordered rehab in L.A., submitted to court-ordered pee tests, the whole bit. The rehab gave her Suboxone and other drugs like Seroquel and gabapentin to wean her off the opioids, but they only served to make her even more high because whatever the normal dose was, she would somehow get five times that amount from the doctors.

When I would go visit her, she didn't even know who I was. I remember sitting with her while she tried to light her cigarette for five full minutes. Unsuccessfully. It was as if it was all happening in slow motion. The cigarette was never closer than a foot away from the lighter.

While in rehab, my mom had decided to get bariatric surgery. Her entire life she had been harassed for being fat. The surgery was something she'd always wanted.

It was a strange time to decide to have surgery in rehab. She wasn't done with her program. I remember worrying that it was a way to stay on medication a little bit longer. I didn't feel she was ready to be sober. If you have any experience with addicts, you'll know that when I questioned her about the timing of the surgery, it turned into a massive fight. That was a dead giveaway. Then she removed me from the guest list at the hospital. In the midst of her addiction, I was a narc to her-I was Pookie (her regular name for me, I was seldom if ever Riley), not a pirate.

I often found myself calling out her attempts to best the system. I would contact the doctors behind her back and tell them that they were overprescribing. But she was Lisa Marie Presley, and so she almost always prevailed, and was furious that I'd tried to intervene. Bending doctors, anyone, to her will was a celebrity phenomenon that she was very aware of. She often told me that the issue with her father, and with Michael Jackson, was that everyone around them always just said yes but of course she didn't see the issue the same way when she was doing it herself. In the throes of her addiction, if you wanted to stop her, you were out. To me she would say, "You don't understand. You're not an addict."

Soon she was out of rehab, but incredibly depressed. She'd been through another separation, and she felt like she had nothing to live for, nothing to look forward to. She was on a bunch of medications that left her numb. All she could really do was sit on the couch and watch TV.

For her to be able to see my sisters, there had to be a court-certified monitor present. I was that monitor, so for my sisters to move back in with her, my mom had to live with me. And as my brother lived with her, I got my brother as a bonus. So my mom, my sisters, and my brother moved into my two-thousand-square-foot house in the Valley. Then my dad moved in, too.

It seemed like it could have been good to have everyone together.

But it felt like the end of things.

We'd had this amazing, colorful, beautiful, abundant, fun, joyful life, but in that house, it took a turn and got unbearably dark, for all of us.

Japan was my brother's favorite country. When Ben and I were on the train to Kyoto one day he said to me, half-jokingly, kind of coyly, "It's so hard because when I do something new, I get really good at it so fast that it becomes uninspiring." Nothing kept his interest long because when he learned to do something, he actually would be good at it. He was one of those people who could annoyingly be great at everything. But he hadn't found the one thing that really grabbed him. He'd wanted to play guitar for a living, he'd taken business courses, he'd trained to be a sushi chef, even got a chef's knife tattooed on one arm, but nothing ever stuck. He was really smart-way more academic than I was. In his mid- twenties, he began to feel pressure to make a choice. I was always trying to help him figure out what to do with his life. "You could move to Hawaii and fish," I'd say, another passion of his. We'd send each other links to houses on Redfin that he might one day buy. His dream was to live a simple life somewhere Hawaii or Japan were his top choices.

But when the conversation would progress, he'd always hit his reality: "I can't leave Mom."

He, like the rest of us siblings, was privy to the tremendously deep sadness and loneliness of her. How she had ended up pushing away virtually everyone and everything she loved and was very much alone. And he'd given himself the responsibility of never leaving her side.

In May 2018, I went to Tokyo to film a movie for Netflix called Earthquake Bird and Ben came with me.

Initially we stayed in the Park Hyatt, the hotel that features in Lost in Translation. I'm not much of a drinker, but on my twenty-ninth birthday, I got way too drunk-I can not handle my alcohol-and threw up over the side of the hotel.

I could hear my parents' voices in my head telling me what a lightweight I was. I probably only had three drinks.

In a family of pirates, that's not necessarily a bad thing to be. My family took pride in their piracy, and they really lived up to it, but as my mother once said when I claimed I was hardcore, "Oh, Pookie, you are so not hardcore."

The next week, we found an apartment to live in.

Ben and I had the most beautiful time in Japan that month. We would wake up every day and head to the sauna or the steam room. Then we'd take a walk to get smoothies and just keep wandering.

I had some yellow Nikes I wore around the city that he was obsessed with. He never wanted anything I had other than those shoes.

I didn't have too much to do in the movie, so there was time. I had an assistant, Shusaku, and he and Ben became best friends. When I did have to work, the two of them would run around the city together. Tokyo is a beautiful place for ceramics, so we went to ceramics classes, the three of us-we made so many pots and bowls and cups, Shu translating for us.

Ben was a foodie. We'd go out to all these incredible omakase restaurants, and he would eat everything and anything. There were dishes that I would not eat-sea urchin, for example --but with the chef right there, I didn't want to be rude, so I'd wait for the chef to look away and then slip whatever it was I couldn't stomach to Ben.

Despite Ben being so into the best food, one of his favorite things to eat were rice balls from 7-Eleven. (In fairness, the food at 7-Elevens in Japan is very good.) We'd take the rice balls to Zushi Beach, a surfer beach about an hour south of the city. We'd climb the mountain to a shrine, me in my bright yellow Nike sneakers-"banana shoes," as Ben called them and eat the rice balls.

Ben would give me a hard time about the shoes every day. "Did you get my banana shoes yet?" he'd ask repeatedly. And I promised over and over that I'd get him a pair.

For a while Ben got heavily into making jewelry.

A few weeks after I started dating the man who would become my husband, Ben Smith-Petersen, we were all in Ireland together. Ben Ben told Ben (my mom later christened the two "Ben Ben" and "Big Ben" to differentiate) that it was obvious that he was going to propose to me-we were children, but we were clearly going to be together-and that he'd make a ring. A few weeks later Big Ben was in Australia visiting his mom. She mentioned that she had some diamonds that she'd taken out of her great-grandmother's ring-she'd intended to repurpose them into something for herself, but she gave him one of them. Back in the States, Ben Ben found a vintage ring with no setting, and set the diamond for Big Ben.

Big Ben then attached the ring to our dog, and told me to call him over. And that's how he-well, technically, the dog- proposed.

Back in L.A., while trying to look after our mother, Ben Ben's own addiction to alcohol was growing.

And as it grew, so did his depression. Though he suffered from anxiety, sober or not, when he wasn't drinking, he was often fine. His depression didn't seem dangerous; he would sometimes go on a bender and he would sometimes do drugs, take Molly for a week and feel the comedown, but after a few days away from it, he was back to normal.

My mom was such a powerful person that whatever she was doing really affected all of us. Our lives were dictated by the tone she was setting, and that tone became very heavy and hopeless. Our mom, the queen, the fiercest of family leaders, had fallen down. I had mistakenly thought she was so strong-minded that nothing could ever truly hobble her. But of course it could. Enough pain can hobble anyone. She'd been addicted to drugs for the better part of a decade and the drugs created a sense of hopelessness that permeated everything. She stopped wanting to do anything. She felt like her life was over. She'd say, "I have nothing-I have no husband, I have no friends, I have no life." She was bottoming out.

Ben Ben was a mama's boy through and through, and he couldn't handle his mama being in pain. They were so close -like Elvis and Gladys-one inextricably tied to the rise and fall of the other, and seeing each other in pain was impossibly hard for them. It wrecked him. What had once felt like a perfect childhood to us gave way to what felt like a nightmare to him. Like many in our family, substances were where Ben found relief, and his alcohol addiction got worse.

Sometimes I'd think, Well, he doesn't seem like he's drinking that much more than other friends of mine. In fact, from that standpoint, he was not even the one I was most concerned about.

We were still very tight, but he didn't tell me how bad he was really feeling. One day he told my mom that he didn't think that he was mentally okay, but she didn't tell me that. And you wouldn't have known unless he told you.

We were all very close, forever cuddling, curled up in bed together. So when it got dark, how could it not affect all of us? All our lives my mother had been leading the way, and none of us could get used to her not having her usual strength. The drugs she stayed on after rehab were dimming her light.

The following year, my mom was able to move into her own house in Calabasas, and my brother and sisters moved in with her.

I swear the house was haunted. It felt cursed. Perhaps it was the intensity of my mother's mood swings.

She wouldn't go more than a few days without seeing me, but I didn't want to be there. The house felt incredibly heavy. My brother could sense it, as could everybody who went there.

Ben Ben eventually realized he was drinking too much, so my mother sent him to rehab.

But when he returned, he was still locked in that dreadful house, watching his mother struggle. She wasn't fully sober, either; she wasn't using opioids, but she was definitely high on the post-treatment cocktail. We would fight about it all the time, and she would get vengeful to preserve her addiction. Otherwise, she would simply sleep on the couch all day. It was really difficult for my brother to see.

Then she experienced a seizure. My brother and her assistant were at home with her at the time, and Ben Ben remained by her side until paramedics arrived.

I showed up that night to care for my sisters. My mother was in the hospital. Ben sat on the couch in solitude. "Are you okay?" I inquired.

"Yep," he replied, as if he were completely tuned out. I was preoccupied with the twins, who had just witnessed the paramedics bring their mother out and were quite distressed, so I didn't have time to check on my brother.

After the seizure, my mother realized she couldn't do it anymore. Although she stayed on mood stabilizers, she was able to truly sober up. One day, she told me, "That's enough. "I really need to change my life."

She had been severely chastened by the seizure, and she had developed a strong phobia of them. When I was around seven years old, I witnessed a man having a terrible seizure on the floor of a Florida mall. My mother couldn't get rid of the picture for months and eventually had to seek therapy for it.

When she told me she'd had it, I remember thinking, Finally. Her addiction was going to be over. I truly believed it was.

However, I saw that my brother's demeanor changed following the seizure. He seemed calmer and was frequently alone in his room. I recall feeling compelled to check on him more than usual since I knew witnessing his mother have a seizure would be horrible for him.

That spooky house in Calabasas had developed a little mold problem, so my mother, Ben, and my sisters stayed in the Beverly Hills Hotel while the problem was resolved. My mother is severely allergic to mold.

During their stay, Ben returned to the house one night to host a birthday party for his girlfriend.

My mother and Ben were messaging back and forth that night. She had noticed something in his mindset that concerned her.

"Will you come back tomorrow? She scribbled, "Come home."

The celebration at the residence lasted till the early morning. Everyone was merrily hanging out downstairs.

Ben walked upstairs around 3:30 a.m.

"Come home," she wrote.

He stated he was only going to get a beer.

Chapter 8: Ben Ben

I swear the house was haunted. It felt cursed. Perhaps it was the intensity of my mother's mood swings.

She wouldn't go more than a few days without seeing me, but I didn't want to be there. The house felt incredibly heavy. My brother could sense it, as could everybody who went there.

Ben Ben eventually realized he was drinking too much, so my mother sent him to rehab.

But when he returned, he was still locked in that dreadful house, watching his mother struggle. She wasn't fully sober, either; she wasn't using opioids, but she was definitely high on the post-treatment cocktail. We would fight about it all the time, and she would get vengeful to preserve her addiction. Otherwise, she would simply sleep on the couch all day. It was really difficult for my brother to see.

Then she experienced a seizure. My brother and her assistant were at home with her at the time, and Ben Ben remained by her side until paramedics arrived.

I showed up that night to care for my sisters. My mother was in the hospital. Ben sat on the couch in solitude. "Are you okay?" I inquired.

"Yep," he replied, as if he were completely tuned out. I was preoccupied with the twins, who had just witnessed the paramedics bring their mother out and were quite distressed, so I didn't have time to check on my brother.

After the seizure, my mother realized she couldn't do it anymore. Although she stayed on mood stabilizers, she was able to truly sober up. One day, she told me, "That's enough. "I really need to change my life."

She had been severely chastened by the seizure, and she had developed a strong phobia of them. When I was around seven years old, I witnessed a man having a terrible seizure on the floor of a Florida mall. My mother couldn't get rid of the picture for months and eventually had to seek therapy for it.

When she told me she'd had it, I remember thinking, Finally. Her addiction was going to be over. I truly believed it was.

However, I saw that my brother's demeanor changed following the seizure. He seemed calmer and was frequently alone in his room. I recall feeling compelled to check on him more than usual since I knew witnessing his mother have a seizure would be horrible for him.

That spooky house in Calabasas had developed a little mold problem, so my mother, Ben, and my sisters stayed in the Beverly Hills Hotel while the problem was resolved. My mother is severely allergic to mold.

During their stay, Ben returned to the house one night to host a birthday party for his girlfriend.

My mother and Ben were messaging back and forth that night. She had noticed something in his mindset that concerned her.

"Will you come back tomorrow? She scribbled, "Come home."

The celebration at the residence lasted till the early morning. Everyone was merrily hanging out downstairs.

Ben walked upstairs around 3:30 a.m.

"Come home," she wrote.

He stated he was only going to get a beer.

I couldn't think about it or hear anything about the arrangements. I recall walking into a room where my mother was smoking a cigarette and looking at various coffins, and I turned and walked right out before she noticed me.

I refused to allow any of it in.

Ben was such an angel that everyone felt it was wrong for him to die. As if a mistake had been made. Even those who only knew him for a short period recognized him as a positive force. You could feel it emanating from him, like light. It felt as if whomever was in charge of this universe had just made a huge mistake.

There were things about my brother that I didn't know until he died, which devastated me because we were so close. For starters, I'd never heard him sing before, but I discovered a voice note on his phone of him singing, and his voice was incredible - deep, gritty, complicated, the voice of someone with undiscovered depths. My mother had a strange connection with music and singing, and it was not promoted in our household. When I was about eight years old, I asked her for singing lessons, and she answered, "I believe if you can sing, you can sing." I don't believe lessons will be effective." Someone had told her this. She didn't want any of her children to have a profession in music to protect them from what she had gone through on her own.

I had no idea Ben had ever considered killing himself. I was devastated that he had not expressed his pain with me. Following his death, my mother and I browsed through his phone together in bed. We were attempting to figure out what had happened, to fit the pieces together. What time did it happen, and who was he speaking to? I discovered an unintentional photo he snapped in the kitchen, most likely while walking back up to his bedroom, just minutes before he died. We discovered a text message sent to my mother a few weeks before his death that stated, "I think something's wrong with me mentally or something like that." I believe I have a mental health condition. It breaks my heart that he realized he might need help only two weeks before he committed suicide. There would have been plenty of room for him to try and heal his anguish. He hadn't even touched the surface of his problems. He hadn't tried and failed; he just hadn't tried yet. He had never gone to therapy. And he'd never attempted suicide before—no overdoses, nothing. There was no scream for rescue. The truth is that he didn't realize the severity of his despair until it was too late, and he went straight for the pistol. The finality of that was so devastating and perplexing.

For months following his death, all we could think about was how this could have been avoided.

The alcohol and drugs had clouded his imagination, preventing him from accessing his soul, light, connection to creation, God, beauty, hope, or whatever the life force is that gives our lives purpose. This was something I observed with my mother over time as well.

But they had not completely extinguished it. To us, he seemed quite alive. He felt joyful. He still maintained his spirit of adventure and fun. Addiction was a part of his life, but his passion for joy and his strong will to live remained intact. Everyone nearby can see him.

However, my mother's addiction had an influence on him as well.

When Ben died, I expected my mother to relapse within a few hours. But she astonished me by staying fully sober to honor him. She aspired to organize her life and help others in some way. She wanted to be of service.

But she was too broken.

My mother kept my brother at home rather than at the morgue. They informed us that if we could take care of the body, we could have him at home, so she kept him at our house on dry ice for a while. My mother needed plenty of time to say goodbye to him, just like she had with her father. And I'd go sit in there with him.

My house has a separate casitas bedroom, where I kept Ben Ben for two months. There is no law in the state of California requiring you to bury someone promptly.

I discovered a funeral home owner who was very compassionate. I informed her that having my father in the house after his death was extremely beneficial because I could spend time with him and chat to him. She stated, "We'll bring Ben Ben to you." "You can have him there."

"Bring him, then," I responded.

We had to keep the room temperature at 55 degrees. I still wasn't sure where I was going to bury him—Hawaii, Graceland, Hawaii, Graceland—which was one of the reasons it took so long. But I got used to caring for him and keeping him around.

I believe it would be terrifying for anyone else to have their son there like that. But not me.

The standard death process is as follows: the person dies, they have an autopsy, a viewing, a funeral, and they are buried. It's all over in four or five days, perhaps a week if you're lucky.

But you don't have much time to comprehend it. I felt really lucky that there was a means for me to continue parenting him, if only for a little longer, until I was comfortable laying him to rest.

My brother had the words Riley and Lisa Marie tattooed on his collarbone and hand a few years before he died. After he died, my mother and I decided to get matching tattoos of his name on the corresponding regions of our bodies. We found a tattoo artist who could match Ben's tattoo of my name, and he then went on to do my mother's tattoo.

We met with the artist in the small courtyard next to the casitas, and my mother was determined that she wanted her tattoo exactly where my brother got his. The artist stated that it was doable, but he would need to know the typeface and location.

"Do you happen to have any photos?"

"No," she replied, "but I can show you."

I glanced at my mother and said, "Are you out of your fucking mind? You have never met this guy before. Don't bring him into the room with my deceased brother.

I knew she recognized my expression, yet she plowed ahead. "He's actually in that room," she explained, pointing to the casitas.

Lisa Marie Presley had just asked this sad man to examine the body of her deceased kid, which happened to be just next to us in the casitas.

I've lived an extraordinarily bizarre life, but this is one of my top five moments.

The tattooist consented to accompany us, bless him, and my mother led us into the casitas, opened the casket, and, in the most matter-of-fact manner possible, grabbed my brother's hand and pointed out the tattoo, discussed its placement, and showed the tattooist where she wanted it on her hand. I stood there, stunned, watching him try to engage in the conversation and pretend everything was fine. I am sure he was thinking, "What the fuck is going on?" But he stayed that day and finished the tattoo correctly, right back at home.

Soon after, we all sensed that my brother no longer wanted his body in this house. "Guys," he appeared to say, "This is getting weird."

Even my mother stated that she could feel him speaking to her, saying, "This is absurd, Mom, what are you doing? "What the fuck!"

Ben's burial was the most traumatic day of my life.

The service took place in Malibu, overlooking the ocean. I believe we broke some Covid guidelines because over a hundred people attended. I was shaking so violently throughout the automobile ride that I believed I'd shatter or have a heart attack.

We followed the hearse and watched as his coffin was carried by the pallbearers, all of his closest boyhood buddies.

The service was as beautiful as it could have been, with everything Ben cherished. We had spent part of our childhoods in Hawaii, so we invited a Hawaiian friend to play Hawaiian music and bless my brother in the customary way. Deepak Chopra led the event. But, as wonderful as it was, I found myself closing my eyes just to get through it. When I opened them, I could hardly see through the tears, and what I did see was a fuzzy image of my young sisters in hysterics, clutching my mother for dear life. So I would close them again.

I simply wasn't there. I had to detach, and my spirit left my body.

I don't recall anything except that I was battling to stay alive. I was hanging on to what Deepak was saying, hoping to find some peace in the moment, but I still felt like I was drowning.

Everyone had written letters to my brother, which were connected to biodegradable balloons and released into the sky while Jeff Buckley's cover of Dylan's "I Shall Be Released" played.

It was simply punishing.

After that, we sent him to Memphis, to Graceland, to be buried alongside his grandfather.

And in his casket, I'd gently placed the yellow Nike sneakers he'd coveted when we were so happy in Japan.

My family stayed in a house together for six months, grieving together. We'd get up and spend the entire day talking about Ben Ben.

My brother and I were really similar. I have always felt that we were twins. We shared our sense of humor, the way we spoke, and even sounded similar. He was only somewhat smarter, wittier, and more cerebral. We've been allowed to ask my parents questions like, "What am I doing here, in this world?" since I can remember, and they've always been willing to talk about it. So, when Ben died, we had a wonderful grief experience that I don't think many people enjoy. We discussed the deeper implications of existence, grief, and love. It was a unique moment in which we all felt a profound connection to something greater than ourselves. My parents, sisters, relatives, and closest friends were all in a Covid and grief pod together. We would take my sisters out to the lawn to sing, paint, and lie under the stars. It was all Ben-centric, a process guided by my mother, who refused to allow us to discuss anything other than her kid. I'm very grateful she did it. If she hadn't set the tone, I might have listened to others who urged me to return to work or pursue some form of escapism to attempt to cope with the loss.

My mom simply answered, "No, we're going through this."

We all agreed that my brother would not have killed himself sober. We all had the impression that the moment he did it, it wasn't what he wanted. Knowing that was difficult for us.

I have never been furious at my brother for what he did. I feel a lot of empathy for him, as well as a deep sadness that he felt like dying was his only option in that moment.

I understand that there is a sense of responsibility in the aftermath of any death, but the guilt associated with suicide is more intense. And because he was my younger brother, I feel personally responsible, as if I failed in my duties as his older sister. Of course, my parents felt it even more strongly than I did.

I recognize that I do not fully grasp the relationship between free will and destiny. Though I feel my brother did not want to die, and though my parents and I wish we had done things differently to prevent this tragedy, and I yearn to see him every day, I have come to believe that everything happens exactly as it should in that time. Ben's death confirmed that for me. I was in the greatest anguish I'd ever felt in my life, but I also had the profoundly transformational experience of surrendering to that avalanche of pain rather than attempting to avoid the sadness. This was a valuable lesson for me:

the only way out is through. To get rid of suffering, you must allow it in.

We are taught not to cry from the minute we are born. We spend a significant portion of our lives attempting to dissociate. Because we are terrified of negative emotions, we try to make ourselves feel better. I, like everyone else, feel uninspired and indifferent about life, as well as broken at times. Life may be excruciatingly difficult and harsh. However, the death of my brother reframed all of those events for me. Ben taught me that every little thing counts, every boring moment, every spark of excitement. All of the suffering.

My brother's death taught me how two, or possibly more, things might be true at the same moment. This has been one of the most profound experiences I have had. Learning to contain joy, suffering, indifference, and hope at the same time.

Sometimes, even today, I'll be doing something and grief's volume will be turned down so I can (barely) function, but most of the time it'll be tuned up to the max and I won't be able to hear anything. A childhood buddy of mine said, "Does it lessen? Is it getting any better?" The answer is no. Today I might be able to take a shower without thinking about it; tomorrow I might be crying in the shower.

Grief is an ever-present emotion.

Days after his death, I sat with his body in the casitas, hoping that he could somehow help me through the grief I was experiencing. That he could give me some advice on this. And on that particular day, I think I could almost hear him remark, "There's a point. "Keep going.

And that sensation has never left me.

After Ben Ben died, I knew my mother would not be able to bear it for long. She did not wish to be here.

When he left the casitas, she chose to spend the rest of her life in sadness. She was no longer interested in discussing anything other than my brother. She would declare that her life was done, that she was only here for her other children, but she was torn since she had three children here on earth and one kid elsewhere.

But she truly astonished us all. For starters, she avoided relapse. She was also more present than she had been in many years. She had some great experiences that allowed her to live her life in ways she hadn't in her addiction years. She went snorkeling, swimming in the water, hiking, and zip-lining during our first trip to Hawaii after Ben Ben died. She desperately attempted to cling on to hope, even if it was like sand through her fingers. I could see her trying. She stated that she was trying. She even attempted to reconnect with some of the folks she had abandoned when she moved to England. She emailed me a photo of herself and one of her old pals at lunch one day—she had phoned a number of them and apologized, almost as if she was attempting to make things right, to finish off any unfinished business here.

And I wish I could create an inspiring, rise-from-the-ashes picture, but the truth is that most days she would sit in her house, smoke a lot of cigarettes, and stare out the window at nothing, everything.

That is how she expressed her pain.

I saw her three times a week, plus every weekend. If she had her way, I would have moved in with her. And if I missed even one hour on a weekend, she'd say, "What could you possibly be doing?"

She considered composing more songs, but she wasn't there yet. She became increasingly determined to help people, particularly mourning parents. She could only feel relieved by assisting others. She wanted to serve others in order to better herself. On Sundays, she would host groups of parents who had also lost children at her residence. She would set out tiny lunches, and she and her grief counselor would lead grief groups. She wrote her first op-ed, about grief. She intended to create a podcast on mourning as a means of finding meaning, and she badly wanted to connect with others who had gone through similar experiences. Nothing else motivated her.

That was what it looked like for my mother to do her best for her other children.

It was gorgeous.

My son insisted that I go to Hawaii. I didn't want to leave. We had a house there, I had lived there, and he loved it; it was his favorite location. He knew I used to go there to recuperate. I suddenly realized I was arranging a trip there, and I told him out loud, "Okay, this is not me, but I'm going. It is you. I am sure it is you. I know you know I don't want to go, but I am going. Then I was there on his death anniversary. It was not a coincidence, and I was careful not to invalidate it.

I got some Vitamin D. I walked a mile every day, which was a significant distance.

I stopped wishing to die every day.

My daughter, Tupelo, was born in August 2022, and for the first week after her birth, my mother would come over and work the night shift so Ben and I could sleep, exactly like I had done for her when she had the twins.

My mother became infatuated with Tupelo; she felt she had a particular connection with her, so she'd come over to my place in Silver Lake and take her away to spend time alone with her. I'd watch through the glass as they went off to sit in the garden, which my mother would refer to as her fairy garden, much as I used to refer to our garden in Hidden Hills as Ben Ben's fairy garden when we were younger. My mother purchased swing sets and toys that filled her home so that Tupelo might sleep over.

But we could all see it, despite all of her remaining love and struggle to survive. We could all sense it coming.

We all knew my mother would die of a shattered heart.

I'm still only fourteen months out. I'm not crying all day every day or hiding myself in my room and not leaving. I've taken baby steps. I can hold a conversation without feeling like I am losing my mind. I can think more clearly now. I was unable to think for quite some time.

How do I heal? By assisting people. One child wrote to Riley, "I didn't commit suicide last night because of what you said it would do to my family and those left behind." Thank you. I'll find another method.

That assisted me. That brought me to my feet.

You're going to have to find something you've never done before, and that will be your mission today, whether you like it or not. And you have to follow through. That is what I am concerned about. It feels incredibly natural to me to respect my Ben Ben while also assisting others by sharing my story with addiction or suicide.

That's where I am now.

Ben's nanny, Uant, who was like a grandmother to him, texted all of us two years ago, saying she was done and that she was going to die. She had nothing wrong with her; she was simply finished. Ben and Riley headed to Florida for one more visit with Grandma.

But nothing occurred. She went on living. She did it a few times, and Ben and Riley got all heated up, but nothing happened.

About six months ago, I was sitting outside alone when I suddenly began thinking about Uant. "I flew all the way to Florida to be with her, go figure...." I heard in my brain. Memories of mom came flooding back to me, songs she used to sing to Ben when he was younger, and I exclaimed aloud to Ben, "Okay, love, I understand it. Something involving Uant. I understand, I hear you. I've got it.

Then I moved on with my day.

Riley arrived the next morning and announced, "Suzanne died last night."

I gave her a look.

"Ben Ben told me yesterday," I stated. "He was telling me something." I had no idea that's what he was saying. I spoke to him aloud yesterday, 'Okay, anything about Uant.'"

I am able to hear him.

I'll never doubt that again.

I saw a picture of myself with my parents yesterday. I was maybe five or six years old. I'm standing between the two of them, and they've each taken my hand.

I glanced at my face as a child and thought, My God, if only someone could have told you what you were going to go through in this life, what you were going to confront. That adorable little blond-haired child in the matching clothing with her mother.

It made me feel overwhelmed.

I'll do that with my own children on occasion. I become quite sad when I look at their faces when they were tiny, before they went through the tragedies they did.

People always said I was depressed after my father died. It left a permanent impact on my face, in my opinion.

However, the melancholy was not captured in this shot. That sad little princess crap hadn't yet appeared.

When he died at the age of nine, the sadness began and has never gone away. Now it's even worse: my eyes are permanently downcast as a result of my anguish. The view is somewhat limited.

I've always wondered why everyone says I seem sad.

And now I understand.

To be completely honest, I don't think my spark will ever return. Grief subsides. It is not something that you can overcome. It is something you have to live with. You adjust to the situation. Nothing about you represents who you were. Nothing regarding how or what I used to think is relevant. The truth is that I can't recall who I was. Someone recently claimed, "I know better than anyone," to which I replied, "No, you don't." You don't know who I am. Because I don't know who the heck I am anymore.

A year and a half ago, the real me, whoever I was, blew up totally.

I have to accept it and let it do its thing, let it take over and engulf me, let it ease up on me, let it step on the gas, step on the brake, step on the gas, step on the brake. I'm simply driving with it.

If I look back on my entire life, I can just lose everything. Try, fail, try again, good, bad, and fail. When I consider how messed up my life has been, I am overwhelmed and begin to cry. Sometimes it feels like there's nothing left, no reason. I feel as if there is nothing I want to accomplish anymore. There's no goal, nothing. Zero. I still have three children, so I battle it, fight it, fight it, fight it. But it is still there, alive and well. It's a lion's roar, and I've got to quiet it down. I'm astonished I'm still living. I can hardly believe I am still standing. Living without Ben feels weird.

But then I can look back on it and say, "Oh, wait, there was that part that wasn't so bad." There was both good and fun over there. I try to add, "It's not all just trash. That is what happened when I met this person. That was good.

Some of it was beneficial.

Despite her efforts to keep it together for my sisters, my mother's health was deteriorating—she had begun to complain that her stomach was constantly bothering her. She would experience feverish episodes. She was trying to keep enthusiastic and hopeful, but behind it all, there seemed to be a rising heartbreak. Despite my repeated appointment scheduling, she would never go to the doctor.

In 2022, she had an illness and had her uterus removed. It was quite challenging for her.

"It held all my babies," she stated.

We all went to Disneyland together on one October day that year. As we were ready to board the bus, she sat down on some stairs and stated that she was not feeling well and was quite queasy. I persuaded her to go to the doctor again, but she did not respond.

What's the goal of an autobiography?

I thought my main goal would be to help others in some way. Or to throw light on a subject. Make a difference somewhere, sometime. I believe others have been through similar experiences, and they may say, "That really helped me."

That would be gratifying.

Or perhaps they will exclaim, "Holy crap, I can't believe you survived that. I cannot believe you are still alive."

When I tell people about my experiences, they tell me I am strong. But that drives me mad because I wonder, what's the point? Throw everything at me, and I will get through it, but for what? What is the importance of strength? It doesn't bother me.

I'm not particularly strong. I am not.

But I am still here. I did not lose my mind, even though I wanted to. And I might have.

I neither relapsed nor died. Or commit suicide, which were three thoughts I had every day for the first eight or nine months after Ben Ben died. I've been vacillating between all three.

But I didn't.

I have two little daughters to care for. I keep my attention on that. My kid was worried about his sisters. It was his primary goal. He sent a few last-minute texts instructing people to keep an eye out and safeguard his sisters. They are not aware of this. I will not tell them until they are older.

I am sure Ben Ben would be furious if I died and joined him.

He would be angry with me in hell or paradise, wherever we went.

Chapter 9: Meditation Garden

My husband and I, together with my parents, went to a Holiday Inn in the Mojave Desert along the 15 freeway the night before my daughter was born to await Tupelo's arrival. Our surrogate was to be induced the next morning. We all had dinner with her--my mother, father, and husband--and then returned to our hotel.

Tupelo was delivered the following morning via C-section. In the midst of it all, I hadn't had time to contact or call my mother, and I had no idea where she was. But when we were walking the baby to her Apgar test, we ran into her. My mother had been looking for us. She wasn't even supposed to be in the area where we met, but she sneaked in and instinctively found her grandchild.

She glanced at Tupelo and said, "Ben Ben brought me to you."

When we got home from the hospital, my parents would work the eight p.m. to one a.m. shift together so Ben and I could get some sleep.

They were a few brief months of bliss, filled with each new tiny blessing in our life. My mother would call Tupelo "our little light," look at her eyes, and say, "Bless her sweet little feisty heart." She resembles a fairy-tale creature—a small fawn."

When my sisters, mom, and I went for a walk outside my mom's house in Calabasas on Thanksgiving, my mother refused to let anybody else hold the baby.

As we strolled that day, we spoke about our Christmas options--Tahoe? Utah? Hawaii? She told the latter, "Yuck! A hot Christmas is my worst nightmare." Every year, she only wanted snow.

I was working in Canada at the time, so I recommended that we all travel to Whistler, British Columbia. She adored that concept. For the next month, I would send her pictures of hotels and activities to do there. She was very excited about it.

I planned everything for her, including flights, hotels, and activities, and the total was exorbitant. But she simply answered, "So what?" "You never know when it will be your last Christmas together."

As the vacation neared, she only needed to renew her passport.

Then came disaster: despite our best efforts, the passport did not arrive on time.

As stupid as it may appear, my mother was quite concerned about not being able to visit Whistler. She longed for a magical retreat, and Whistler had come to symbolize an ideal, a dreamland. When it fell through, I swear something shifted. She appeared to have accepted something, as if she would no longer be able to enjoy the joy she had once felt here.

In addition to her feeling ill in Disneyland, there was an unusual energy near the conclusion of 2022. Unusual things kept happening to her health. She got an infection and had to go to the hospital in November. She was given painkillers, which concerned me. I didn't want to question her or police her about it since I knew it would lead to another major conflict. So I trusted her to take what she needed without abusing the drugs. (After her death, I heard from her toxicology report that she had taken a therapeutic amount, which made me very proud of her.)

Things began to cascade. She was frequently complaining about her stomach and feeling queasy. She drank a lot of Pepto-Bismol, which was always beside her bed. I could tell my sisters were concerned, too—they'd frequently ask me, "Is Mama going to be okay?" I would answer yes, but I didn't believe it. Perhaps my sisters were also aware.

After Christmas, which turned out to be our final holiday together, we all headed to Santa Ynez to ring in 2023. It wasn't Whistler—it was actually a spot we went every New Year's—so it was more gloomy than exhilarating, but at least we were together. My mother, sisters, and I took horseback rides through the gorgeous valley. I observed my mother gradually establish communication with the horse, feeling it out and learning its rhythm. She was so in tune with horses that she could create a relationship with even the grumpiest of them. It was moving to see her intuit a horse's individuality.

On New Year's Eve, we found ourselves at a honky-tonk pub where a band was performing covers. At one point, they performed a country version of "Suspicious Minds," and my mother walked up to praise them. The lead singer was arrogant—he probably liked looking at himself in the backs of spoons—and he barely spoke to my mother, which she found amusing.

When she returned to our table, she laughed. "Arrogant son of a bitch," she exclaimed.

I responded: "I don't think he knew who you were, Mom."

After we finished watching the band, my sisters retired to their rooms, and my mother and I slipped off to an area near the nonsmoking hotel restaurant, giggling like teens hiding from their parents and lighting up. I had stopped smoking years ago, but I wanted to smoke this cigarette with my mother. My dad eventually came around the corner and lit a cigarette as well.

We three stood under the roof, smoking and avoiding the light rain.

As we smoked, my mother exclaimed, "Ugh, that baby-I can't handle her! She fills me up and knocks me out."

"I know, sweet Sawney," my father murmured. (My mother's word "fawn" has become Sawney in our funny common language.)

In that moment, I realized how grateful I was to still have both of my parents. I did not take it for granted.

That was the last time I truly went out with my mother until we had dinner in Los Angeles on January 8, which happened to be her father's birthday, just her, myself, my husband, and my pals, as was customary. She was unusually silent and aloof, immersed in her own world. I continued to try to involve her in the conversations, but she glanced at me and said, "I'm going home."

Her expression was one of despair and resignation. I was concerned.

My spouse and I led her to the car. She appeared incredibly soft, almost empty, yet my mother was not a soft person.

Something had left her.

A few days later, I returned to Vancouver, where I was filming a show. I found myself texting her more than usual, but she was less receptive. My worry grew.

On the morning of January 12, my mother texted my father, "Can you please help? My stomach hurts worse than ever. "Could you bring Tums?"

I had a lovely morning with the baby. I texted my mom the day before, and she didn't respond, which was unusual for her.

When my father called, I knew something horrible had occurred.

"It's your mom," he responded, "and it's not looking good." My heart has stopped.

By the time he arrived with the Tums she had requested, the housekeeper had discovered her on the floor.

"They think she's had a heart attack," he told me. "She is in an ambulance right now. "They're attempting to revive her."

I went straight to the airport and boarded the first aircraft back to Los Angeles. My dad and spouse texted me throughout the vehicle ride, and then again when I was in the air.

"They're in the hospital now.... She is still alive. They've revived her... She now has a pulse. They're conducting a scan to determine what happened...

I brought my best friend with me on the plane to assist with Tupelo. At some point during the journey, my acquaintance told me, "People have heart attacks all the time."

I looked at her and said, "I don't think she'll make it through this. I do not think she wants to."

My husband and I, together with my parents, went to a Holiday Inn in the Mojave Desert along the 15 freeway the night before my daughter was born to await Tupelo's arrival. Our surrogate was to be induced the next morning. We all had dinner with her--my mother, father, and husband--and then returned to our hotel.

Tupelo was delivered the following morning via C-section. In the midst of it all, I hadn't had time to contact or call my mother, and I had no idea where she was. But when we were walking the baby to her Apgar test, we ran into her. My mother had been looking for us. She wasn't even supposed to be in the area where we met, but she sneaked in and instinctively found her grandchild.

She glanced at Tupelo and said, "Ben Ben brought me to you."

When we got home from the hospital, my parents would work the eight p.m. to one a.m. shift together so Ben and I could get some sleep.

They were a few brief months of bliss, filled with each new tiny blessing in our life. My mother would call Tupelo "our little light," look at her eyes, and say, "Bless her sweet little feisty heart." She resembles a fairy-tale creature—a small fawn."

When my sisters, mom, and I went for a walk outside my mom's house in Calabasas on Thanksgiving, my mother refused to let anybody else hold the baby.

As we strolled that day, we spoke about our Christmas options-- Tahoe? Utah? Hawaii? She told the latter, "Yuck! A hot Christmas is my worst nightmare." Every year, she only wanted snow.

I was working in Canada at the time, so I recommended that we all travel to Whistler, British Columbia. She adored that concept. For the next month, I would send her pictures of hotels and activities to do there. She was very excited about it.

I planned everything for her, including flights, hotels, and activities, and the total was exorbitant. But she simply answered, "So what?" "You never know when it will be your last Christmas together."

As the vacation neared, she only needed to renew her passport.

Then came disaster: despite our best efforts, the passport did not arrive on time.

As stupid as it may appear, my mother was quite concerned about not being able to visit Whistler. She longed for a magical retreat, and Whistler had come to symbolize an ideal, a dreamland. When it fell through, I swear something shifted. She appeared to have accepted something, as if she would no longer be able to enjoy the joy she had once felt here.

In addition to her feeling ill in Disneyland, there was an unusual energy near the conclusion of 2022. Unusual things kept happening to her health. She got an infection and had to go to the hospital in November. She was given painkillers, which concerned me. I didn't want to question her or police her about it since I knew it would lead to another major conflict. So I trusted her to take what she needed without abusing the drugs. (After her death, I heard from her toxicology report that she had taken a therapeutic amount, which made me very proud of her.)

Things began to cascade. She was frequently complaining about her stomach and feeling queasy. She drank a lot of Pepto-Bismol, which was always beside her bed. I could tell my sisters were concerned, too—they'd frequently ask me, "Is Mama going to be okay?" I would answer yes, but I didn't believe it. Perhaps my sisters were also aware.

After Christmas, which turned out to be our final holiday together, we all headed to Santa Ynez to ring in 2023. It wasn't Whistler—it was actually a spot we went every New Year's—so it was more gloomy than exhilarating, but at least we were together. My mother, sisters, and I took horseback rides through the gorgeous valley. I observed my mother gradually establish communication with the horse, feeling it out and learning its rhythm. She was so in tune with horses that she could create a relationship with even the grumpiest of them. It was moving to see her intuit a horse's individuality.

On New Year's Eve, we found ourselves at a honky-tonk pub where a band was performing covers. At one point, they performed a country version of "Suspicious Minds," and my mother walked up to praise them. The lead singer was arrogant—he probably liked looking at himself in the backs of spoons—and he barely spoke to my mother, which she found amusing.

When she returned to our table, she laughed. "Arrogant son of a bitch," she exclaimed.

I responded: "I don't think he knew who you were, Mom."

After we finished watching the band, my sisters retired to their rooms, and my mother and I slipped off to an area near the nonsmoking hotel restaurant, giggling like teens hiding from their parents and lighting up. I had stopped smoking years ago, but I wanted to smoke this cigarette with my mother. My dad eventually came around the corner and lit a cigarette as well.

We three stood under the roof, smoking and avoiding the light rain.

As we smoked, my mother exclaimed, "Ugh, that baby-I can't handle her! She fills me up and knocks me out."

"I know, sweet Sawney," my father murmured. (My mother's word "fawn" has become Sawney in our funny common language.)

In that moment, I realized how grateful I was to still have both of my parents. I did not take it for granted.

That was the last time I truly went out with my mother until we had dinner in Los Angeles on January 8, which happened to be her father's birthday, just her, myself, my husband, and my pals, as was customary. She was unusually silent and aloof, immersed in her own world. I continued to try to involve her in the conversations, but she glanced at me and said, "I'm going home."

Her expression was one of despair and resignation. I was concerned.

My spouse and I led her to the car. She appeared incredibly soft, almost empty, yet my mother was not a soft person.

Something had left her.

A few days later, I returned to Vancouver, where I was filming a show. I found myself texting her more than usual, but she was less receptive. My worry grew.

On the morning of January 12, my mother texted my father, "Can you please help? My stomach hurts worse than ever. "Could you bring Tums?"

I had a lovely morning with the baby. I texted my mom the day before, and she didn't respond, which was unusual for her.

When my father called, I knew something horrible had occurred.

"It's your mom," he responded, "and it's not looking good." My heart has stopped.

By the time he arrived with the Tums she had requested, the housekeeper had discovered her on the floor.

"They think she's had a heart attack," he told me. "She is in an ambulance right now. "They're attempting to revive her."

I went straight to the airport and boarded the first aircraft back to Los Angeles. My dad and spouse texted me throughout the vehicle ride, and then again when I was in the air.

"They're in the hospital now.... She is still alive. They've revived her... She now has a pulse. They're conducting a scan to determine what happened...

I brought my best friend with me on the plane to assist with Tupelo. At some point during the journey, my acquaintance told me, "People have heart attacks all the time."

I looked at her and said, "I don't think she'll make it through this. I do not think she wants to."

Made in United States
Orlando, FL
13 November 2024

53877023R00085